SOMETHING MORE

—A DEVOTIONAL DIMENSION
FOR THE JOSEPH-DANIEL CALLING —

by

Morris E. Ruddick

PRESS

ALSO AVAILABLE BY MORRIS RUDDICK

THE JOSEPH-DANIEL CALLING: Facilitating the Release of the Wealth of the Wicked

GOD'S ECONOMY, ISRAEL AND THE NATIONS: Discovering God's Ancient Kingdom Principles of Business and Wealth

THE HEART OF A KING: The Leadership Measure of the Joseph-Daniel Calling

TABLE OF CONTENTS

DEDICATION

In the mid-nineties, Carol and I experienced a horrible tragedy. Our 30 year-old daughter Trisha, a committed mission practitioner, was brutally murdered. To compound this terrible event, she was murdered by her husband, a man we had come to love and trust.

Months after her death, we were faced with attending Trisha's murder trial. I had no desire to be there; no desire to be exposed to and relive the awful details of her death and the betrayal that had had such an impact on our entire family. Despite our embracing a forgiveness that could only have been the result of the supernatural grace of God, we knew our presence in the courtroom was not at option.

Simultaneously, my consulting work at that time, no doubt due to the distractions and heaviness tied to her loss and the developments of the ensuing investigation, had wound down to a dribble. There were more bills on my desk than I had funds in the bank.

It was in that context and state of mind that I was praying, asking God for some relief from the oppression tied to the courtroom encounter that lay before us. Deep in prayer, the Lord spoke a clear word to me that initially seemed out of context, saying, "Morris, do you know that you're a rich man?"

Momentarily puzzled, I knew His reference was not to what I had in my bank account at the time. Then, without a great deal of experience with visual-type visions, I began having one. Like a panorama before me, I began seeing face after face after face of friends in prayer for us. And as I viewed those the Lord accounted as riches for me, I knew, despite what lay ahead, that everything was going to be alright.

The Lord has indeed blessed me richly with the friends I have. Among them are those who have come to the plate, as my inner circle, each in their own special way, in making a tangible impact in the fulfillment of the calling on my life. We recently had a small gathering of these special friends led by my wife Carol, Bill and Rita Bartlett, Judy Haynes and Ann Woodruff. Attending were Peter and Faith Yesner, Don Shooster, Ron and Paul O'Dell, David and Marie Works, Wayne Newcomb, Jeff Ahern and Marco Leardina. There are a handful of others who weren't at this gathering, but for each of those mentioned and those not mentioned, who I have come to account as my greatest "riches," I simply want to say "thank God for you and may the gift of your extremely valued friendships be multiplied back to you."

This dedication would not be complete without mention of the couple who have pastored us since the last half of the eighties. Wally and Marilyn Hickey have been our friends and greatest encouragers and supporters in prayer. They model, in the way they have walked out their ministry, what the Scripture refers to as the balance between Spirit and Truth. I have been honored to have served as a volunteer in what soon-thereafter became a pastoral position in their ministry; followed by 19 years as a member of their board.

ACKNOWLEDGEMENTS

For their generous and careful review of this manuscript, along with the wisdom imparted that is in keeping with who they each are, I want to express my deepest appreciation to Judy Haynes, Barbara Fox and Wayne Newcomb.

Then for those who have so faithfully upheld us in prayer, I fall short in finding words capable of describing the depth of my gratefulness.

Finally, but certainly not last, I want to acknowledge my wife Carol, whose patience with my times apart to seek the Lord, as well as my unorthodox mid-watch schedules of prayer, has gone beyond the call of duty.

PREFACE

Walking out a call of God begins at a level described in the Book of Hebrews as milk. Milk is palatable, easily digested and provides a sense of comfort. Maturity on the other hand is described as meat. Meat requires more work and cannot be digested until development progresses to a certain level.

The milk mode comes primarily from the preaching and teaching of others.

The meat or proactive mode to maturity comes from a direct interaction with the Holy Spirit through deep immersion into God's Word and prayer. The meat mode takes time, dedication and commitment. The transition takes place when the believer departs from absorbing information to entering a vibrant, ongoing interactive flow with the Spirit.

This is a proactive process that leads into the pathway described by Jesus as having its entrance at the narrow gate.

Paul's conversion began with him already having a substantive grasp of the Scripture. Despite that, he described his pathway to the meat-mode in Galatians 1:16-18. Paul wrote the Galatians that following his dramatic Damascus road experience, he did not confer with flesh and blood, nor even go to the Apostles in Jerusalem; but went away to Arabia where God revealed His plan for him to bring the gospel to the Gentiles. The suggestion is that for maturity, we must move beyond the comfort levels of the milk to that something more, where our regular spiritual sustenance is on meat.

The path to Joseph the Patriarch's high calling began when God gave him two dreams. Despite one of the Western church's most misinterpreted conclusions about Joseph; that for the next thirteen years, God had to work on Joseph's character, there was something a great deal more. Character was the secondary benefit to Joseph entering the flow of the Spirit which actuated him to being positioned to reverse the curse brought on his household by the wayward digressions of his brothers.

God, through Joseph, was redeeming the destiny of His chosen people. It was during those thirteen years in Egyptian slavery and prison that Joseph developed a proactive interaction with God that resulted in him boldly telling the baker and wine-taster that *"interpreting dreams is God's business, so tell me your dreams."* It was during that time that Joseph's heart aligned with God in such a way, that when promoted to sit along side Pharaoh, he not only accomplished God's intentions, but became as a father to Pharaoh.

For the heroes of faith like Paul and Joseph, entering that dimension of the Spirit took something more. It is that something more that is the focus of this book. This devotional is designed as a supplement to my first three books, "The Joseph-Daniel Calling," "God's Economy, Israel and the Nations," and "The Heart of a King." It targets those called with a high calling to bring transformation and to disciple nations.

The Process

Romans 1:17 describes our spiritual progress as going from faith to faith. It is a process. In my case, early in my walk with the Lord, I began spending time each day reading God's Word and praying. I used a method of interactive journaling to record questions and considerations that occurred to me in prayer about the new pathway I was walking.

Then, through missionary friends we spent time praying with at the time, I was exposed to a robust, nine-chapter a day Bible-reading program. I sampled and followed this program for a time; then developed my own version that I used for the next twenty some-odd years.

After a time of almost uninterrupted success, we hit some uncharted waters. I was grounded in God's Word, but operating beyond my natural abilities. My pastor imparted some advice that I didn't understand at the time, but that I heeded. His advice was to take three or four days alone with the Lord and do nothing but pray in the Spirit. I found that easier said than done, but I pressed through and emerged changed. That change might best be described as the gateway to the bridge crossing the dividing asunder between soul and spirit. It provided and provides the release tied to the gifts Paul describes in Romans 12 that previously had only comparatively been trickles operationally.

Then there came a time when we relocated and found ourselves in a community that was teeming with witch covens. The spiritual atmosphere we had entered was subtle and it was deadly. It didn't take long before I recognized that if we were to survive, I would need something more than the daily hour and a half program of God's word and prayer that I had been following.

That something more proved to be a booklet by Marilyn Hickey titled "Speak the Word." In short, this potent little booklet includes personalized scriptures that provide proclamations concerning wisdom, joy, abundant life, safety, release from fear, family, unconditional love, relationships and those in authority.

I was being assaulted by the curses of some very high-level leaders from these satanic covens. The oppression was beyond anything I had ever experienced. So, before I began reading the Bible each morning; I would read these personalized scriptures aloud. Some days I'd read them through *out loud* twice; some days three times; and when things were especially heavy, I'd do it four times. I eventually memorized the scriptures in this booklet; and found it to be the potent difference in establishing a shield against aggressive forces of darkness.

So, the process evolved from a foundation of maintenance in which I spent quality time each day in God's Word, followed by interactive prayer that was journaled and reviewed. The basics were then augmented by praying in the Spirit and a practice of what began with Marilyn Hickey's booklet: a progressive memorization program. Over time, the employment of these practices of seeking the Lord and His heart began to give birth to unexpected, supernatural dimensions bearing on my calling.

God's Unexpecteds

1995 seemed to mark a transition into a time when the Lord would initiate agendas for me to follow. It was in that year that I discovered what an Internet search engine was. With part of my background being in the media, I wanted to know if this medium was being used by believers for Kingdom purposes. Specifically, I was interested in whether anyone was using the Internet to "address strategic-level issues impacting the Body globally" through intercession.

The story that unfolded can be read in my "God's Economy" book, but in short what transpired was the birthing of an Internet-based ministry in which I began writing articles bearing on "strategic-level issues impacting the Body globally." We call it the Strategic Intercession Global Network (SIGN www.strategicintercession.org). SIGN has also evolved into a blog bearing the name of the Strategic Issues Global Network (http://strategicissuesnetwork.blogspot.com).

As I embraced the charge of seeking the Lord for the substance of these strategic-level issues and writing articles bearing on matters close to His heart, the Lord clearly let me know that I was not to read or listen to any teachings on these topics by others who may have been addressing them. In other words, there was to be no analysis or consensus. God wanted revelation.

Despite the process of my walk with Him advancing aggressively from faith to faith, I found myself seriously questioning the confidence I had to hear from my prayer closet and put together articles on what, at the time, were relatively virgin topics that would be read in those early days by several hundred people.

Yet, that was exactly what the Lord expected me to do. My concerns likewise were unfounded. As I proceeded into this new arena, the Lord was very faithful in guiding and making clear the focus of what was coming from my time with Him. The "ban" on reading or listening to what other leaders were saying about these topics extended until year 2000, when at His instruction, I compiled a group of articles from this process which became "The Joseph-Daniel Calling" book.

It was during this new focus of defining strategic issues in the late nineties that the Lord prompted me to add a new dimension to this process. I began prayerfully compiling scripture to memorize each year. Combined with a year-end time of reconsecration and prayer for what the Lord would be unfolding in the upcoming year, absorbing a new swath of scripture began to give greater clarity to the path I was walking.

The "absorption" of these scriptures provided a depth in grasping their meaning that began being reflected in the SIGN posts I was writing. Likewise, I began realizing a theme that came from each annual group of scriptures memorized that carried a prophetic dimension to what took place for me that year.

The dynamic no doubt parallels what is intended for leaders by Deuteronomy 17. Deuteronomy 17 reflects a mandate to the one who sits on the throne as king. In short, they must keep a copy of God's word with them wherever they go and read it daily. Tradition indicates that the kings originally were charged with writing out, by hand, the entire Torah and memorizing it. Those bearing the true calling of todays priestly kings, the Josephs and Daniels, carry the same responsibility.

The Approach

The substance of this book reflects twelve years of scriptures that bear on my own calling as a modern-day Joseph-

Daniel pioneer. It provides a robust approach to nurture the calling of a generation of leaders whose roles are integrated with what the Lord is doing through the marketplace.

License has been taken with the scriptures in each chapter to maximize their impact. In some cases they have been personalized, in others a passage has been condensed, in still others vague wording clarified. In no cases, were meanings changed. For each scripture, the reference is given for readers desiring to review the translations available for themselves. In two instances, in Chapter Two, I have included personal words I have received in prayer and have noted them as such.

There is ample flexibility for the use of these scriptures. For most, after an initial review, I suggest taking a chapter each month and reading them aloud daily. There will be some, who find a hunger for "something more" than this approach; who may commit to memorizing them. The value of doing so will bear untold fruit.

The appendix includes a chart with instruction to guide the reader into the program comprising nine chapters of the Bible each day. There is also a prayer for the persecuted church, as well as a cleansing prayer, the function of which when combined with personal communion, I describe as pressing the spiritual default button.

Stewardship

Years ago, I was deeply touched by the message of a book titled "Dedication and Leadership" (Douglas Hyde, Notre Dame Press, 1992). Written by a former communist activist with the "Daily Worker," who had been converted to Christianity, it portrays the observation of the need for the Western church to at least match the zeal of communist zealots. The effort of this book reflects the "something more" needed to go beyond matching that zeal.

The issue is stewardship. Some have estimated that more than half the scriptures on righteousness are within the context of stewardship. What this book's approach addresses is the stewardship of your calling. Solomon's Proverbs give keen focus to the counterpoints of wisdom and stewardship: the fool and the sluggard. This devotional/manual is not for those with priorities focused on their comforts and the lust of the flesh. If taken seriously and acted on; it will prove to be the meat of maturity leading to that "something more" than might ever come from natural efforts.

I have long carried a great burden for those with the Joseph-Daniel calling. It is a high calling; one that cannot be trifled with or obtained with ease. The cost matches the calling. The substance of my previous books has frequently been described as meat. The substance is aligned with the calling; as Jesus made it clear that *"many would be called, but few chosen."*

For those chosen, the Joseph-Daniel calling will indeed require "something more." The "something more" will be the maturity that prevails. It will be the mark of true Kingdom leadership. This effort is not for those needing to be spoon fed, nor those drawn by good intentions or ambitions, or any other notion of man, apart from God's call.

May the ones called to put their hands to the plow, pierce the veil to realize the mark of this high calling.

INTRODUCTION

THE FINE LINE

Reaching for "something more" will entail a grasp of the "fine line." The "fine line" extends beyond the portals of the narrow gate referenced in two of the Gospel accounts. It involves those moving into what some refer to as the deeper things of the Spirit. It impacts those called to do something beyond the ordinary. It is those who, in their times with the Lord, go beyond what most others will ever "see." It will be those serving as pioneers, paving the way for others. It will be those who have connected to something in the spirit, and by faith are hanging on.

For those penetrating these thresholds, the fine line entails increases in the delicacy and precision required to maneuver and advance. This is not to be confused with a prideful perfectionism. It involves progressive subtleties in the distinctions between operating in the soulish realm and in the spiritual. For much being given, much will be required.

The more deeply we move into the spirit realm, the more we will recognize this fine line between operating in faith and operating in foolishness; between operating in the supernatural and operating in la-la land.

It is the fine line that marks the difference between being strong in faith and forcing an issue. It is the fine line that distinguishes between being controlling and being able to speak into a person's life. The fine line is being a trusted vehicle to speak forth the Word of the Lord, but not having the words we deliver being tied to an egotistical need for acceptance. The fine line differentiates between faith and presumption. The fine line is the separation in recognizing and correctly interpreting deep truths, and over-spiritualizing. The fine line divides the flow of the Spirit and the subtle compulsions of the flesh.

This fine line is "the dividing asunder between soul and spirit" spoken of in Hebrews. It is the difference between operating by human effort and seeing the results from entering His rest.

The bottom line for the fine line of whether we stay the course is the poise of our soul. It is the issues of the heart. It requires an absolute openness to be REAL in the presence of the Lord. The cost of the "secret place" of His presence is a heart that can stand before Him without any covert issues; without any "secret" places or hidden agendas of the soul.

There have been some within prophetic circles who have referenced the idea of the "wounded prophet." Without any unkindness intended, whether in the prophetic or any other arena of spiritual leadership, you can't expect to move forward or to travel the distance with unresolved baggage. Jesus described the narrow path of those bearing the Kingdom mantle. Those who press into the depths; yet overlook what the Bible refers to as the issues of the heart are treading in hazardous territory.

This is not a case for unfruitful, wheel-spinning introspection. It's about learning to genuinely operate as Galatians 2:20 suggests, and as Paul admonishes the Corinthians that we should daily die to self. You can't hurt a dead man.

Such is the mystery. It is the exchange of His Life for ours. It is an exchange that means we are unfazed by the circumstance or situation. The key to proceeding on this path is to insure that we guard our hearts, that we speak truth in our own hearts, and that the issues of our hearts are open and real between us and the Lord. It is foundational to the relationship.

David's Promotion and Poise of His Soul

David, known as a man after God's heart emerged from an extended time of great pressures and tribulations, to a time in which the promises came forth. He had rest from his enemies, as he was now the king with great influence and prosperity. Then there emerged the episode with Bathsheba. This familiar story when Nathan came forth to confront David includes some profound subtleties. There is no doubt of David being convicted of his sin. However, strong clues of David's weakened relationship with the Lord were evidenced, as Nathan imparted the word of the Lord to him.

In 2 Samuel 12:10 Nathan addresses the core issue in David's downfall. The passage reads that *"the sword will not depart from your house, because YOU HAVE DESPISED ME."* David "despising" the Lord is a major departure from the one who had previously been known as consistently having *"sought the Lord."*

God's Word through Nathan reminded David that the Lord had given David his master Saul's house and his wives, as well as all of Judah and Israel. Then it went on to say that if that had not been enough for David, the Lord would have given David *"much, much more."*

How could one who had been so faithful, for so long, have slipped to the point to where he was described as despising the Lord?

The implication is that David had become preoccupied and distracted in giving the Lord first priority. That preoccupation and distraction came within the context of the very position God had put him in; to bless Him and to use him. While the Bible isn't specific on this matter, it implies that his downfall began with the priority David gave to His time with the Lord. He had lost his intimacy with Him.

David had come to the pinnacle of the promises and blessings God had spoken to him about years prior. Yet, at issue in his downfall, was the place in his heart He was now giving the Lord. It bears on the subtle encroachment of the pride of life, the love of the world and the lust of the flesh upon God's anointed.

This would not have happened if David had been giving heed to the poise of his soul. The clear night that David gazed out and saw Bathsheba and was tempted was not an event. It was the culmination of a subtle process. It was a process in which David lost focus and failed in that which had once been his greatest strength: of being one whose soul was always "poised toward the Lord." He was riding the momentum of his past successes. At that juncture the Lord described the condition of David's heart as "despising the Lord." David had lost that place in the crucible. No doubt, David had begun believing his own press releases. David had survived the years of persecution. He had arrived.

Thank God David could face the truth and that he knew how to repent! Thank God he knew what it meant to be *"weak, though anointed."*

The Transition into Promotions

There are many key players within the Body who, like David, have been waiting for years for what the Lord has promised. They have been faithful in that waiting process. The time is fast approaching when the fullness promised will be upon them. Many, like Joseph, are poised to be promoted to sit along side of Pharaoh. Some, like David, will see the end of pressures and persecutions and be elevated to positions of prestige and influence and authority. They will embrace privileged positions prepared for them by the Lord. They are privileged positions to enable them as the chosen, to be used mightily in the accomplishment of key God-ordained agendas. They will be bearing mantles of high trust.

The Apostle Paul provides a key to the before, the during, and the after of the transition. Paul said that regardless of his situation, that he had learned contentment. He wrote the Philippians and told them that in whatever "condition" he found himself, abased or abounding, he had learned contentment. Why? It was because his orientation was dependent on the

Lord, not on his circumstance. Paul also understood and lived the truth in Proverbs 16 that the one *"who rules his own spirit, is mightier than the one who takes a city."*

There are some within the Body, who have experienced years of preparation for the calling God has for them; with the time of His high purpose at hand. It is a time not unlike that described for Queen Esther, *"for such a time as THIS!"*

In his letter to the Romans (Romans 12:2), Paul admonishes them *"not to be conformed to the world."* The Phillips translation expresses that verse well by saying *"don't let the world squeeze you into its mold."*

While we all know that, this truth is critical to those about to be promoted; those making the transition from the called to the chosen. With the promotions will be changes in venue and function that need to be recognized. They won't be recognized if that central factor operating prior to the promotion is in any way relaxed: the poise of our hearts toward Him, together with the priority given to our time with Him.

That means maintaining the highest priority to the time spent regularly immersing ourselves in His Word. That means giving focus to the time given to personal worship and fellowship with Him. It means honing the spontaneity of prayer and a heart that seeks Him first as the foundation to the high calling.

The deception with the promotion is the idea of having arrived. If anything, the process that led to the promotion, time with Him, is going to be more important than ever. The faithfulness that takes one through the time of waiting has got to be at the forefront in addressing and accomplishing the agendas God has entrusted to those promoted. It represents the fine line.

The Fine Line for Those Being Promoted

The fine line is maintaining that edge. The fine line is speaking truth in our own hearts, as outlined in the 15th Psalm. The fine line is constantly guarding our hearts with all diligence as we are admonished in Proverbs 4. The fine line is insuring that every thought is brought captive to the obedience of Jesus. The fine line is sacrificing our ego and personal agendas so that the love of God can flow through us; so we can be instruments of HIS purpose.

The fine line is operating according to the Kingdom mysteries. To lead we must serve. True greatness is based on humility. We bless those who curse us. The fine line is not natural. But then, it is no longer our lives we are living. The fine line is daily avoiding spiritual staleness and never being satisfied with anything less than revival reigning in our hearts. It is never being willing to accept anything less than that wonderful consciousness of His presence.

The gifts may be flowing. Lives may be touched. Miracles no doubt will come forth in great measure. Incredible things will be accomplished for the Kingdom. Yet if we ever relinquish that poise of the soul toward Him and that time with Him, the result will be for naught. We will be like a loud gong or a clanging cymbal. Regardless of our circumstance or position; whether we are facing promotion or simply allowing the Spirit to draw us more deeply into the agendas He is entrusting us with, let us maintain that place in Him spoken of by David as *"weak, though anointed."*

The narrow gate is followed by the narrow path. The narrow pathway is a life guided by the Spirit. It's what being a God-pleaser is all about. It is a life that cannot in any way be guided by the pride of life, the love of the world, or the lusts of the flesh. Nor can it be relinquished to our feelings, or our brilliant ideas, or our self-righteousness, or the approval of man, or any other factor other than us operating in total oneness and harmony with the Master. That's the fine line. And for those crossing the boundary between the called and chosen, that's the bottom line.

SECTION I

THE FOUNDATION

CHAPTER 1

THE PATHWAY

1. The Lord enlarges my path under me so my feet do not slip. (Ps 18:36) Behold I shall prosper, be exalted and lifted up, and shall be very high. So shall I startle many nations: kings shall shut their mouths because of me, for that which has not been told them they shall see and that which they have not heard they shall understand. (Is 52: 13,15)
2. God is going to gather and heap up, that He may give to me what is good before Him. Eccl 2:26 Then I shall again discern between the righteous and the wicked, between one who serves God and one who does not serve Him. Malachi 3:18 I know that You O God, can do everything, and that no purpose of Yours can be withheld from You. Job 42: 2
3. What I decide will be done and light will shine on my ways. Job 22:28 Then I will see and be radiant, my heart shall thrill and rejoice, because the abundance of the sea shall be turned to me and the wealth of the nations shall come to me. (Is 60:5) I shall eat the wealth of nations and in their riches God will establish me. Instead of shame I will have a double portion of blessing, instead of dis-honor, I shall rejoice in that which God supplies; there-

fore in my land I shall possess a double portion; mine shall be an everlasting joy. (Is 61:6)

4. The Lord foils the signs of false prophets and makes fools of diviners. He confirms the word of His servant and performs the counsel of his messengers. (Isa 44:24,25) I am His battle axe and weapon of war: with me He breaks nations in pieces, with me He destroys kingdoms and strongholds. (Jer. 51:20) I walk not in darkness for it is given unto me to know the mysteries of the kingdom. The Lord instructs me and teaches me in the way that I should go: He guides me with His eye (Matt 13:11; Rom 1:19; Ps 32:8).

5. Lord, You soar on the wings of the wind. Out of the brightness of Your presence bolts of lightning blaze forth. The LORD thunders from heaven; the voice of the Most High resounds. You scatter my enemies, bolts of lightning rout them. You reach from on high and take hold of me; You draw me out of deep waters and rescue me. 2 Sam 22:11

6. God has commanded my strength. Strengthen O God, what you are doing for me. (Ps 68:28) For the Lord gives victory to me wherever I go and is winning a name for me (II Sam 8:6,13). For the Lord is with me and I am a successful man and everyone sees that the Lord is with me and has made all that I do to prosper. (Gen 39:2,4)

7. For the pillars of the earth are the Lord's, and He has set the world upon them. He will guard the feet of His saints, but the wicked shall be silent in darkness. For by strength, no man shall prevail. The adversaries of the Lord shall be broken in pieces; from heaven He will thunder against them. I Sam 2:8

8. By His Spirit He adorned the heavens; His hand pierced the fleeing serpent. These are but the mere edges of His ways, and how small a whisper we hear of Him; but the thunder of His power who can understand! (Job 26:14)

9. God is my strength and power, and He makes my way perfect. He makes my feet like the feet of deer, and sets me on high places. He teaches my hands to make war,

so that my arms can bend a bow of bronze. You have also given me the shield of Your salvation; Your gentleness has made me great. You have enlarged my path under me; so my feet do not slip. I have pursued my enemies and destroyed them; neither do I turn back again till they are destroyed. And I have destroyed them and wounded them, so that they could not rise; they have fallen under my feet. For You have armed me with strength for the battle; You have subdued under me those who rose against me. You have also given me the necks of my enemies, so that I destroyed those who hated me. (II Sam 22:33-39)

10. Lord, You are ridding Yourself of this constant grumbling against me. (Num 17:5) A man's gift makes room for him and brings him before great men. (Prov 18:16) The man who excels in his work will stand before kings, he will not stand before unknown men. (Prov 22:29). I will be enriched in everything with all bountifulness. (II Cor 9:11) In everything, I am enriched in Him in all speech and all knowledge. (I Cor 1:5). The Lord has given me favor in the sight of the Egyptians and they grant me whatever I request. (Ex 12:36)

11. You hide me in the secret place of Your presence from the conspiracies of men and in your dwelling you keep me safe from the strife of tongues (Ps 31:20). Although the wicked may draw their swords and bend their bows, to bring down and slay those whose ways are upright; their bows will be broken and their swords will pierce their own hearts. (Ps 37:14, 15) Lord, You have cut asunder every wicked scheme by which Satan has tried to entrap, enslave, enshroud and defeat me (Ps 129:4)

12. Lord, You are sending Your terror before me, and are throwing into confusion all those confronting me, and You are making all my foes turn from me [in flight]. And You are sending hornets before me, which are driving out my enemies from before me. Exodus 23: 27-30 For the accuser is cast down.

13. Wealth and riches shall be in my house and my righteousness endures forever. My horn shall be exalted in honor. The wicked will see it and be vexed. They will gnash their teeth and slink away, their hopes being thwarted (Ps 112:3,9,10)

14. God is restoring the years the locusts have eaten, and we shall eat in plenty and be satisfied, and praise the name of the Lord our God, who has dealt wondrously with us, and we shall never again be put to shame. (Joel 2:25,26)

15. Yours O Lord is the greatness and the power and glory and the victory and the majesty, indeed everything that is in the heavens and earth is Yours. Yours is the dominion and You do exalt Yourself as head over all. Both riches and honor come from You and You do rule over all, and in Your hand is power and might; and it lies in Your hand to make great, and to strengthen. Now therefore my God, I thank you and praise Your glorious Name. (I Chron 29: 11-13)

16. In righteousness I am established, I am far from oppression, for I do not fear and terror does not come near me. If anyone stirs up strife, it is not from the Lord. Whoever stirs up strife with me shall fall because of me. (Is 54:14,15) No weapon formed against me shall prosper, and I shall confute every tongue that rises against me in judgment. This is my heritage as a servant of the Lord and my vindication from the Lord. (Is 54:17)

17. The purposes of the Lord in me and through me will be established. (Prov 19:21) I cry out to God most high, Who always fulfills His purposes for me. (Ps 57:2) Declaring the end from the beginning, saying His purpose will be established, and He will accomplish His good pleasure; calling the eagle from the east, the man of His purpose from a far country. Truly He will bring it to pass. (Is 46:10,11)

18. As their (those I minister to) faith grows, I shall be, within my sphere enlarged even more (II Cor 10:15). But I will

not boast beyond my measure, which God has apportioned to me. (II Cor 10:13-18)

19. And he prayed, Lord open his eyes that he may see. And he saw; the mountain was full of the chariots of fire. And those who are with us are more than those against us! (II Kings 6:16,17) Lift up a standard on the bare hill, raise your voice to them. Enter the doors of the nobles; for the Lord has commanded His consecrated ones, He has even called His mighty warriors. The Lord is mustering His army for battle. (Isaiah 13: 3-4)

20. Blessed be the name of the Lord God forever and ever, For wisdom and might are His. And He changes the times and the seasons; He removes kings and raises up kings; He gives wisdom to the wise and knowledge to those who have understanding. He reveals deep and secret things; He knows what is in the darkness, and light dwells with Him. (Daniel 2:20-22)

CHAPTER 2

THE CALLING

1. For He that touches me or my work touches the apple of His eye. (Zech 2:8) With God I do valiantly for it is He who treads down my foes. (Ps 108:13) The scepter of wickedness shall not rest on the land of the righteous. (Ps 125:3) Take counsel, execute judgment, for the extortioner is at an end. Devastation ceases; the oppressors are consumed. In mercy the throne will be established. (Is 16:3)

2. You have delivered my soul in peace from the battle that has been against me. (Ps 55:18) You are my lovingkindness and my fortress, my high tower and my deliverer, my shield and the One in whom I take refuge, Who subdues these people under me. (Ps 144: 2) Now is the accepted time. (II Cor 6:2)

3. I do not call to mind the former things nor ponder the things of the past. Behold the Lord is doing a new thing. NOW it is springing forth. Will you not be aware of it? He is making a roadway in the wilderness and rivers in the desert; to give drink to His chosen people. (Is 43:18,19) Mercy and truth will not forsake me, I bind them around my neck and write them on the tablet of my heart, and so I find favor and high esteem in the sight of God and man. (Prov 3:3,4)

4. For the Lord my God will help me, therefore I shall not be confounded, therefore have I set my face like a flint and I know I shall not be ashamed. (Is 50:7) The Lord is faithful, Who shall establish me and keep me from evil. (II Thes 3:3) For the Lord shall be my confidence and shall keep my foot from being taken. (Prv 2:26) Being confident of this very thing; He Who began a good work in me will perform it. (Phil 1:6)

5. So awake, cloth yourself with strength; O, arm of the Lord, an everlasting joy will crown your head; gladness and joy will overtake you. So awake and clothe yourself with strength. (Is 51:9) Upon praying the seventh time, Elijah said, I see a cloud as a man's hand. Go prepare your chariot and leave before the rains prevent you. (I Kings 18:44) For the eyes of the LORD run to and fro throughout the whole earth, to show Himself strong on behalf of those whose heart is loyal to Him. (2 Chron 16:9)

6. I call unto You, and You answer me and show me great and mighty things, which I previously did not know. (Jer 33:3). Lord, You have made the heavens and earth by Your great power and outstretched arm. Nothing is too hard for You! (Jer 32.17) I told them of the hand of God strong upon me, and of the king's words. So they said, let us rise up and build, and they set their hands to do this good work. (Neh 2:18)

7. I do not fear, for from the first day that I set my mind to understand and humbled myself before God, my words have been heard; and help, provision and enablement have come and continue to come because of my words. (Dan 10:12) From six calamities He will rescue me; in seven no harm will befall me. In famine He will ransom me from death, and in battle from the stroke of the sword. I will be protected from the lash of the tongue, and need not fear when destruction comes. (Job 5:19) A throne of destruction cannot be allied with me for I am Yours O Lord. (Ps 94:20)

8. Because I wait upon the Lord my strength is renewed; I mount up with wings as eagles; I run and am not weary, I walk and am not faint. (Is 40:31) Because I know my God, I will be strong and do exploits. (Dan 11:32) I shall eat the bread from Asher and be rich, and I shall yield and dispense royal dainties. (Gen 49:20)

9. I do remember the Lord my God, for it is He who has given me the power to get wealth that He might establish His covenant. (Deut 8:18) ALL these blessings shall come upon me and overtake me because I obey the voice of the Lord my God. (Deut 28:2) The Lord my God blesses me as He has promised me, and I shall lend to many nations, but shall not borrow and I shall rule over many nations, but they shall not rule over me. (Deut 15:6)

10. Yet now I take courage. For once again, in a little while the Lord will shake the heavens and the earth and the sea and the dry land, and he will shake the nations, so that treasurers of all the nations will come in and fill this house with the splendor of the Lord. (Haggai 2:4) The Lord is making me abundantly prosperous in all the work of my hands, the Lord takes delight in prospering me because I take delight in obeying the voice of the Lord my God. (Deut 30:9) It is the blessing of the Lord that makes rich and He adds no sorrow to it. (Prov 10:22) In a very little while our fruitful field shall be a forest. (Is 30:17)

11. I will call nations I do not know and nations that didn't know me shall run to me because the Lord my God has exalted me. (Is 55:5) For the wealth of the seas will be brought to me and the riches of the nations will come. My gates will stand open continually, so that men may bring to me the wealth of the nations. You are the Lord. You will do this swiftly, SUDDENLY and I will be called a minister of our God and I will feed on the wealth of nations. (Is 60:1) I have been sent to reap that which I have not

worked for. Others have done the labor and I have come into their gain. (John 4:38)

12. I do not cast away my confidence, for it has great reward. I have developed endurance, that I might do the will of God, and I will receive the promise (Heb 10:35,36) The Lord is with me and lets none of my words fall to the ground. (I Sam 3:19) The Lord is making me the head and not the tail and I will always mount higher and not decline. (Deut 28:13) The latter splendor of this house shall be greater than the former; and in this place the Lord will give prosperity. (Haggai 2:6)

13. He is about to shake the heavens and the earth and to overthrow the thrones of kingdoms. He is about to destroy the strength of the kingdoms of the nations and overthrow them. On that day He will take me and make me His signet ring for he has chosen me. (Haggai 2:20) The LORD knows the days of the upright, and their inheritance shall be forever. I shall not be ashamed in the evil time, and in the days of famine I shall be satisfied. (Ps 37: 18-19)

14. God provides me with every blessing in abundance, so I may always have enough of everything and may provide in abundance for every good work. (II Cor. 9:8) I will rejoice in the sphere of influence I walk into, but immediately begin looking beyond it, lest it overwhelm me. (Personal word: 1978) The Lord will make me a thousand times more. (Deut 1) I do not stagger at the promises of God through unbelief; but am strong in faith, giving glory to God; being fully persuaded that what He promises, He is also able to perform. (Rom 4:20,21)

15. Just as in the days of Joseph and Daniel, God will bring out mighty works at my hand. As I am led into the midst of the world, kings, rulers, leaders will be converted and humbled. I shall work beside them and be given authority and my counsel will be heeded for their good. (Personal word: 1976) In all matters that kings and leaders inquire

of me, they will find me ten times better than all the wisdom of the world within their realm. (Daniel 1:20)

16. As I extend my soul to the hungry and reach out to the oppressed, then my light shall dawn in the darkness, and my darkness shall be as the noonday. The LORD will guide me continually, and satisfy my soul in drought, and strengthen my bones; I shall be like springs of water, whose waters do not fail. (Isa 58:10, 11) He will pour out overwhelming, overflowing blessings that I won't even be able to contain. (Mal 3:10)

17. For God has commanded me. I am strong and coura-geous. (Jos 1:6,7,9) I am blessed because I trust in the Lord. I am like a tree planted by the rivers of waters that stretches out its roots to the stream; I fear not the heat when it comes, my leaves stay green; in the year of drought I know no distress, but bear fruit. (Jer 17:7) I shall not grow weary in well doing, for I will reap because I will not faint. (Gal 6:9)

18. I have waited patiently for the Lord; He inclined to me and heard my cry. He put a new song in my mouth, a song of praise to my God. He has multiplied His won-drous deeds and thoughts toward me, to which none can compare. I delight to do His will. (Ps 40: 1,3,5,8) I walk in the gentleness of wisdom: which is pure, gentle, rea-sonable, full of mercy and good fruits; unwavering and without hypocrisy. (James 4:13)

19. Because of God's love for me, He will deliver me, He will set me on high, because I have known His name. I call upon Him and He answers me. He is with me in trouble; He delivers me and honors me; and with long life He satisfies me and gives me His salvation. (Ps 91:14-16) For every plant not planted by the Lord will be rooted up. (Matt 15:13)

20. Who am I, O Lord God, and what is my family that You should have brought me as far as I have come: Yet even this You consider too little, O Lord, for Your servants sake and in keeping with Your purpose you have done

these great things. O God there is no one like You and no God but You, just as I have always understood. In keeping with Your Word, O Lord, bring about what You have promised. (I Chron 29:14)

CHAPTER 3

PENETRATING DARKNESS

1. In the time of the end, many shall be purified and refined, but the wicked shall do wickedly and none of the wicked shall understand; but the wise shall understand. So I will go my way and find rest, and arise to my inheritance. (Dan 12:10-13) Those who are wise shall shine like the brightness of the sky, and those who lead many to righteousness, like the stars forever and ever. (Daniel 12:3)
2. Lord, You make me wiser than my enemies; I have more understanding than all my teachers, for Your Words are my meditation. I understand more than the ancients, because of Your Word. (Ps 119: 98-100) The steps of a good man are ordered by the LORD, and He delights in his way. Though he fall, he shall not be utterly cast down; for the LORD upholds him with His hand. (Ps 37:23-24)
3. Lord, You have been with me wherever I have gone and cut off my enemies from before me. You will make my name great. You will give me rest from all my enemies. You will raise up my descendents after me, those who come forth from me. Your lovingkindness shall not depart from me. (2 Sam 7:9)
4. For the angel of the Lord encamps around those who fear Him and delivers them. (Ps 34:7) You give Your angels charge over me to keep me in all my ways. In

their hands they bear me up, lest I dash my foot against a stone. I shall tread upon the lion and the cobra. You have set Your love upon me, and will deliver me and will set me on high, because I have known Your name. (Ps 91:11-16)

5. The angel touched me and strengthened me and said, "O man greatly beloved, fear not! Peace be to you; be strong, yes, be strong!" When he spoke I was strengthened and said, "Let my lord speak for you have strengthened me." (Dan 10: 18,19)

6. The days are near when every vision will be fulfilled. For I the Lord will speak what I will and it will be fulfilled without delay. For the rebellious shall see that I will fulfill whatever I say declares the Lord. When the people say the visions he sees are for many years from now say, this is what the Lord says, "None of My Words will be delayed any longer, whatever I say will be fulfilled." (Ez 12:22)

7. There was famine in the land and the LORD appeared to Isaac and said: "Dwell in this land, and I will be with you and bless you and perform the oath which I swore to Abraham your father." Then Isaac sowed in that land, and reaped in the same year a hundredfold; and the LORD blessed him. So he began to prosper, and continued prospering until he became very prosperous. (Gen 26:1-3, 12, 13)

8. Pharaoh said, "Can we find such a one as this, a man in whom is the Spirit of God? Inasmuch as God has shown you all this, there is no one as discerning and wise as you. You shall be over my house, and all my people shall be ruled according to your word; only in regard to the throne will I be greater than you. I am setting you over all the land of Egypt." (Gen 41: 38-41)

9. He sent a man before them; Joseph; who was sold as a slave. They hurt his feet with fetters, he was laid in irons. Until the time that his word came to pass, the word of the LORD tested him. (Ps 105:17-19) Joseph

is a fruitful bough by a well; his branches run over the wall. The archers have bitterly grieved him, shot at him and hated him. But his bow remained in strength, and the arms of his hands were made strong by the hands of the Almighty. By Adonai who will help you, and by the Almighty who will bless you; with blessings of heaven above, blessings of the deep that lies beneath, blessings of the breasts and of the womb. Your blessings have excelled the blessings of your ancestors. They shall be on the head of Joseph. (Gen 49:22-26)

10.   Thus says the Lord to these dry bones: Surely I will cause breath to enter into you and I will put sinews and flesh upon you, and you shall live. Prophesy to the breath, O son of man and say, Thus says the Lord GOD: "Come from the four winds, O breath, and breathe on these slain, that they may live." So I prophesied and sinew and flesh came upon them and breath came into them, and they lived, and stood on their feet, an exceedingly great army. (Ezek 37:4-10)

11.   Jabez was more honorable than his brothers, so Jabez called on the God of Israel saying, "Oh, that You would bless me indeed, and enlarge my territory, that Your hand would be with me, and that You would keep me from evil, that I may not cause pain!" So God granted his request. (I Chron 4: 9, 10)

12.   In returning and rest am I saved; in quietness and in confidence is my strength. (Is 30:15) Lord, You turn my mourning into joy, and You comfort me, and make me rejoice from my sorrow. (Jer 31:13) By Your Word, O Lord, I have stayed far from the paths of the destroyer. (Ps 17:4) For to me belong wisdom and might, to me belong counsel and understanding. (Job 12:13) Lord you equip me with every good thing to do your will, working in me that which is pleasing in Your sight (Heb 13:2). You strengthen me with all power, according to Your glorious might. (Col 1:29)

13. Lord, who may abide in your tent? Who may dwell in your Holy Hill? He who walks with integrity and works righteousness and speaks truth in his heart; who does not slander with his tongue, nor does evil to his neighbor, nor takes up a reproach against his friend; in whose eyes a reprobate is despised, but who honors those who fear the Lord. He swears to his own hurt and does not change, He does not put out his money at interest, nor does he take a bribe against the innocent. He who does these things will never be shaken. (Psalm 15)

14. The LORD, who delivered me from the paw of the lion and from the paw of the bear, will deliver me from the hand of this Philistine. You come to me with a sword and a spear. But I come to you in the name of the LORD of hosts, the God of the armies of Israel, whom you have defied. This day the LORD will deliver you into my hand, and I will strike you and take your head from you. And I will give the carcasses of the Philistines to the birds of the air, that all the earth may know that there is a God in Israel. Then all shall know that the LORD does not save with sword and spear; for the battle is the Lord's, and He will give you into our hands. (I Sam 17:37, 45-47)

15. Do not be afraid! Don't be discouraged by this mighty army, for the battle is not yours, but Mine. Go out against them. You will not even need to fight. Take your positions; then stand still and watch the Lord's victory. I am with you. Do not be afraid or discouraged. Go, for the LORD is with you!" (2 Chr 20:15-17) He does not restrain them when His voice is heard! He does great things which we cannot understand. (Job 37:4,5)

16. I do not fret because of evildoers, nor am I envious of the workers of iniquity. For they shall soon be cut down like the grass, and wither as the green herb. I trust in the LORD, and do good; I dwell in the land, and feed on His faithfulness. I delight myself in the LORD, for He gives me the desires of my heart. I commit my way to the LORD, I trust also in Him, and He shall bring it to

pass. He shall bring forth my righteousness as the light, and my justice as the noonday. I rest in the LORD; wait patiently for Him; I do not fret because of him who prospers in his way, because of the man who brings wicked schemes to pass. I cease from anger, and forsake wrath; I do not fret; it only causes harm. Evildoers shall be cut off; but those who wait on the LORD shall inherit the earth. (Psalm 37:1-9)

17.   Make haste O God, to deliver me. Let them be ashamed and confounded who seek my life. Let them be turned back and confused who desire my hurt. Let those who seek You rejoice and be glad in You. Make haste to me O God! You are my help and my deliverer. O Lord, do not delay. (Ps 70:1)

18.   For my obedience has become known to all. Therefore the Lord is glad on my behalf; but He calls me to be wise in what is good, and simple concerning evil. For the God of peace will crush Satan under my feet shortly. (Rom 16:19-20) A curse without cause will not alight (Pr 26:2)

19.   Elijah came near and said, "LORD, let it be known this day that You are God in Israel and I am Your servant, and that I have done all these things at Your word. Hear me, O LORD, that this people may know that You are the LORD, and that You have turned their hearts back to You." Then the fire of the LORD fell. (I Kings 18: 36-38)

20.   Lord, You will do nothing without revealing Your secrets unto Your servants the prophets. (Amos 3:7) In You I have boldness and access, with confidence, through faith in You. (Eph 3:12) Lord, You have fortified my gates against all enemies, and blessed my household. You send peace within my borders and satisfy me with plenty of the finest wheat. You send your commands across the earth; look how swiftly Your Word goes forth. (Ps 147:13-15)

SECTION II

THE FOCUS

CHAPTER 4

THE MAJESTY

1. O Lord, our Lord, how majestic is Your name in all the earth, Psalm 8:1, 3 I will extol You, my God, O King; and I will bless Your Name forever and ever. Every day I will bless You. Lord, You are gracious and merciful, slow to anger and great in loving-kindness. All Your works shall give thanks to You and Your godly ones shall praise You. Psalm 145:1, 2, 8-10

2. You are worthy, our Lord and our God, to receive glory and honor and power; for You created all things, and for Your pleasure they are and were created. And You O Lamb, are worthy to take the book, and to break its seals, for You were slain, and purchased for God with Your blood, men from every tribe and tongue and people and nation. And You have made them to be kings and priests to our God; and they will reign upon the earth. Revelation 4:11; 5:9-10

3. Blessed are You, my rock; and exalted are You, the God of my salvation, You Who execute vengeance for me, You subdue people under me. You deliver me from my enemies and lift me above those who rise against me. So I give thanks to You among the nations and sing praises to Your name. You give great deliverance to Your ser-

vant, and show lovingkindness to Your anointed. Psalm 18:46-50

4. God is our refuge and strength, a very present help in trouble. Therefore we will not fear even if the earth should move and the mountains be carried into the midst of the sea; though its waters roar and be troubled, though the mountains shake. There is a river whose streams shall make glad the city of God, the holy place of the tabernacle of the Most High. God is in the midst of her and she shall not be moved; God shall help her just at the break of dawn. The nations raged, the kingdoms were moved; He uttered His voice, the earth melted. The LORD of hosts is with us; The God of Jacob is our refuge. Psalm 46:1-7

5. Have mercy upon me, O God, according to Your lovingkindness; according to the multitude of Your tender mercies, blot out my transgressions. Wash me from my iniquity and cleanse me from my sin. You desire truth in the inward parts, and in the hidden part You will make me to know wisdom. Purge me with hyssop, and I shall be clean; wash me, and I shall be whiter than snow. Make me hear joy and gladness. Hide Your face from my sins, and blot out all my iniquities. Create in me a clean heart, O God, and renew a steadfast spirit within me. Do not cast me away from Your presence, and do not take Your Holy Spirit from me. Restore to me the joy of Your salvation, and uphold me by Your generous Spirit. Then I will teach transgressors Your ways, and sinners shall be converted to You. Psalm 51:1-13

6. The law of the LORD is perfect, converting the soul; the testimony of the LORD is sure, making wise the simple; the statutes of the LORD are right, rejoicing the heart; the commandment of the LORD is pure, enlightening the eyes; The fear of the LORD is clean, enduring forever; the judgments of the LORD are true and righteous altogether. More to be desired are they than gold, yes, than much fine gold; sweeter also than honey and the hon-

eycomb. Moreover by them Your servant is warned, and in keeping them there is great reward. Who can understand his errors? Cleanse me from secret faults. Keep Your servant also from presumptuous sins; let them not have dominion over me. Then I shall be blameless, and I shall be innocent of great transgression. Let the words of my mouth and the meditation of my heart be acceptable in Your sight, O LORD, my strength and my Redeemer. Psalm 19:7-14

7. Unless the LORD had been my help, my soul would have dwelt in the abode of silence. When my foot slips, Your mercy will hold me up. In the multitude of my anxieties, Your comforts delight my soul. Shall the throne of iniquity, which devises evil by law, have fellowship with You? But the LORD has been my defense, and my God the rock of my refuge. He has brought on them their own iniquity, and shall cut them off in their own wickedness; the LORD our God shall cut them off. Psalm 94: 17-23

8. O LORD God, to whom vengeance belongs, shine forth! Rise up O Judge of the earth; render punishment to the proud. LORD how long will the wicked triumph? They utter arrogance and speak insolent things and boast in themselves. They break in pieces Your people and afflict Your heritage. They slay the widow and the stranger, and murder the fatherless. He who planted the ear, shall He not hear? He who formed the eye, shall He not see? He who instructs the nations, shall He not correct? Blessed is the man whom You instruct and teach out of Your law. That You may give him rest from the days of adversity, until the pit is dug for the wicked. For the LORD will not cast off His people, nor forsake His inheritance. Psalm 94:1-14

9. My enemies turn away in retreat; they are overthrown and destroyed. For you have judged in my favor; from Your throne, you have judged with fairness. You have rebuked nations and destroyed the wicked.. The Lord is a shelter for the oppressed, a refuge in times of trouble.

Those who know Your Name trust in You. For You, O Lord, have never abandoned anyone who searches for You. For You who avenge murder care for the helpless. You do not ignore those who cry to You for help. For the wicked have fallen into the pit they dug for others. They have been caught in their own trap. Lord, You are known for Your justice. The wicked have trapped themselves in their own snares. Psalm 9

10. Bless the LORD, O my soul; and all that is within me, bless His holy name! Bless the LORD, O my soul, and forget none of His benefits: Who forgives all your iniquities, Who heals all your diseases, Who redeems your life from destruction and crowns you with lovingkindness and tender mercies, Who satisfies your mouth with good things, so that your youth is renewed like the eagle's. The LORD executes righteousness and justice for all who are oppressed. He made known His ways and acts to the children of Israel. The LORD is merciful and gracious, slow to anger, and abounding in mercy. Bless the LORD, you His angels, who excel in strength, who do His word, heeding the voice of His word. Bless the LORD, all you His hosts, you ministers of His, who do His pleasure. Bless the LORD, all His works, in all places of His dominion. Bless the LORD, O my soul! Psalm 103:1-8, 20-22

11. The earth is the Lords and all it contains, the world and those who dwell in it. For You have founded it upon the seas and established it upon the rivers. Who can ascend to Your hill and stand in Your holy place? He who has clean hands and a pure heart, who has not lifted up his soul to falsehood, nor sworn deceitfully. He shall receive a blessing from You and righteousness from You, the God of his salvation. Psalm 24:1-5

12. This is the generation of those who seek You, who seek Your face - even Jacob. Lift up your heads, O gates, and be lifted up, O ancient doors, that the King of glory may come in! Who is the King of glory? The Lord strong and

mighty, the Lord mighty in battle. Lift up your heads, O gates, and lift them up, O ancient doors, that the King of glory may come in! Who is the King of glory? The Lord of hosts, You are the King of glory. Psalm 24:6-10.

13. Lord, You reign and I rejoice; clouds and darkness surround You; righteousness and justice are the foundations of Your throne. The heavens declare Your righteousness and all people have seen Your glory. You are the Lord most High over all the earth. You are exalted far above all gods. I am glad in You and give thanks to Your Holy Name. Psalm 97:1,2,6,9,12. Lord, You have made known Your salvation. You have revealed Your righteousness in the sight of all nations. You have remembered Your lovingkindness and faithfulness to the house of Israel. All the ends of the earth have seen Your salvation. Lord, You are coming to judge the earth. You will judge the world with righteousness and the people with equity Psalm 98:2,3,9

14. All nations whom You have made shall come and worship before You, O Lord; and they shall glorify Your name. For You do great and wondrous deeds; You alone art God. Teach me Your way, O Lord; and I will walk in Your truth; unite my heart to fear Your name. Psalm 86:9-11

15. With the merciful You will show Yourself merciful; with a blameless man You will show Yourself blameless; with the pure You will show Yourself pure; and with the devious You will show Yourself shrewd. For You will save the humble people, but will bring down haughty looks. For You will light my lamp; the LORD my God will enlighten my darkness. For by You I can run against a troop, by my God I can leap over a wall. As for God, His way is perfect; the word of the LORD is proven; He is a shield to all who trust in Him. Psalm 18: 25-30

16. Lord, You bring us out of our distresses. You calm the storm, so that its waves are still. Then we are glad because we are quiet; so You guide us to our desired haven. Psalm 90:14-17 Satisfy us early with Your mercy,

that we may rejoice and be glad all our days! Let Your work appear to Your servants, and Your glory to their children. And let the beauty of the LORD our God be upon us, and establish the work of our hands for us; yes, establish the work of our hands. Psalm 107:29-30

CHAPTER 5

WISDOM

1. The Lord stores up sound wisdom for the upright; He is a shield to those who walk in integrity, preserving the way of His godly ones. Then you will discern righteousness and justice and equity and every good course. 2:7-9 My son, do not forget my law. Let your heart keep my commands; for length of days and long life and peace they will add to you. Let not mercy and truth forsake you; bind them around your neck, write them on the tablet of your heart. So find favor and high esteem in the sight of God and man. Trust in the LORD with all your heart; lean not on your own understanding; in all your ways acknowledge Him, and He shall direct your paths. 3:1-6 Happy is the man who finds wisdom, and gains understanding; for her proceeds are better than fine gold, and all the things you may desire cannot compare with her. Length of days is in her right hand, in her left hand, riches and honor. V13-18

2. Keep your heart with all diligence, for out of it spring the issues of life. Put away from you a deceitful mouth, and put perverse lips far from you. Ponder the path of your feet, and let all your ways be established. 23,24,26 Remove your way far from seduction, and do not go near the door of her house, lest you give your honor to others,

and your years to the cruel one; lest aliens be filled with your wealth, and your labors go to the house of a foreigner. 5:8-10

3. The fear of the LORD is the beginning of wisdom, and the knowledge of the Holy One is understanding. For by me, your days will be multiplied, and years of life will be added to you. If you are wise, you are wise for yourself, and if you scoff, you will bear it alone. 9:10-12 Whoever hides hatred has lying lips, and whoever spreads slander is a fool. In the multitude of words sin is not lacking, but he who restrains his lips is wise. 10: 18-19 The lips of the righteous feed many. The blessing of the LORD makes one rich, and He adds no sorrow with it. V21-22.

4. He who is devoid of wisdom despises his neighbor, but a man of understanding holds his peace. A talebearer reveals secrets, but he who is of a faithful spirit conceals a matter. Where there is no counsel, the people fall; but in the multitude of counselors there is safety. 11:12-14 The merciful man does good for his own soul, but he who is cruel troubles his own flesh..V17-19 The generous soul will be made rich, and he who waters will also be watered. v29 He who troubles his own house will inherit the wind, and the fool will be servant to the wise of heart. The fruit of the righteous is a tree of life, and he who wins souls is wise. V29-31

5. A good man obtains favor from the LORD, and the root of the righteous cannot be moved. 12: 1,2 The mouth of the upright will deliver them and the house of the righteous will stand. A man will be commended according to his wisdom. V6-8 A fool's wrath is known at once, but a prudent man covers shame. V16 There is one who speaks like the piercings of a sword, but the tongue of the wise promotes health. V18 The hand of the diligent will rule, for diligence is man's precious possession. V24,27. Anxiety in the heart of man causes depression, but a good word makes it glad. V25

6. A man shall eat well by the fruit of his mouth, and he who guards his mouth preserves his life. The soul of the diligent shall be made rich. 13:1-4 By pride comes nothing but strife, but with the well-advised is wisdom. 13:10 Hope deferred makes the heart sick, but when the desire comes, it is a tree of life. V12 A prudent man acts with knowledge, but a fool lays open his folly. V16 He who walks with wise men will be wise, but the companion of fools will be destroyed. V20 A good man leaves an inheritance to his children's children, but the wealth of the sinner is stored up for the righteous. V22

7. In the mouth of a fool is a rod of pride, but the lips of the wise will preserve them. 14:3 Go from the presence of a fool, when you do not perceive in them the lips of knowledge. The wisdom of the prudent is to understand his way, but the folly of fools is deceit. V7,8 The simple believes every word, but the prudent considers well his steps. A wise man fears and departs from evil, but a fool rages and is self-confident. V14-16 V19 He who is slow to wrath has great understanding, but he who is impulsive exalts folly. What is in the heart of fools is made known. 29, 33 Righteousness exalts a nation, but sin is a reproach to the people. The king's favor is toward a wise servant. 34,35

8. A soft answer turns away wrath, but a harsh word stirs up anger. The tongue of the wise uses knowledge rightly, but the mouth of fools pours forth foolishness. 15:1,2 A wrathful man stirs up strife, but he who is slow to anger allays contention. V18 V20 Without counsel, plans go awry, but in the multitude of counselors they are established. A man has joy by the answer of his mouth. The way of life winds upward for the wise. V27. The fear of the LORD is wisdom, and before honor is humility. V33

9. The preparations of the heart belong to man, but the answer is from the LORD. Commit your works to the LORD, and your thoughts will be established. 16 1,3 When a man's ways please the LORD, He makes even

his enemies to be at peace with him. V7 A man's heart plans his way, but the LORD directs his steps. V9. Righteous lips are the delight of kings, they love him who speaks what is right. 28 He who is slow to anger is better than the mighty, and he who rules his spirit than he who takes a city. 32

10. An evildoer gives heed to false lips; a liar listens eagerly to a spiteful tongue. 17:4 The beginning of strife is like releasing water; therefore stop contention before a quarrel starts. 14 A merry heart does good, like medicine, but a broken spirit dries the bones. 22 He who has knowledge spares his words, and a man of understanding is of a calm spirit. Even a fool is counted wise when he holds his peace; when he shuts his lips, he is considered perceptive. 26

11. A fool has no delight in understanding, but in expressing his own heart. 18:2,4 The name of the LORD is a strong tower; the righteous run to it and are safe. V8 He who answers a matter before he hears it, it is folly and shame to him. V13 A man's gift makes room for him and brings him before great men. V16 Better is the poor who walks in his integrity than one who is perverse in his lips and is a fool. Also it is not good for a soul to be without knowledge, and he sins who hastens with his feet.

12. The foolishness of a man twists his way, and his heart frets against the LORD. 17 The first one to plead his cause seems right, until his neighbor comes and examines him. 19:1-3 He who gets wisdom loves his own soul; he who keeps understanding, will find good. V8 The discretion of a man makes him slow to anger and his glory is to overlook a transgression. What is desired in a man is kindness. V21-23

13. It is honorable for a man to stop striving, since any fool can start a quarrel. 20:3 Counsel in the heart of man is like deep water, but a man of understanding will draw it out. Who can find a faithful man? The righteous man walks in his integrity; his children are blessed after him.

V5-7 Plans are established by counsel; by wise counsel wage war. Whoever curses his father or his mother, his lamp will be put out. V20.

14. The spirit of a man is the lamp of the LORD, searching all the inner depths of his heart. V27 The king's heart is in the hand of the LORD, He turns it wherever He wishes. 21:1 The plans of the diligent lead to plenty, but those of everyone who is hasty, to poverty. V5 Whoever guards his mouth and tongue keeps his soul from troubles. V23 There is no wisdom or understanding or counsel against the LORD.

15. A good name is to be chosen over great riches, loving favor than silver and gold. By humility and the fear of the LORD are riches and honor and life. He who sows iniquity will reap sorrow, and the rod of his anger will fail. He who has a generous eye will be blessed. 22:1-10 Make no friendship with an angry man, and with a furious man do not go, lest you learn his ways and set a snare for your soul. V25 Do you see a man who excels in his work? He will stand before kings; he will not stand before unknown men. V29

16. Do not speak in the hearing of a fool, for he will despise the wisdom of your words. 23:9 Through wisdom a house is built, and by understanding it is established; by knowledge the rooms are filled with precious riches. For by wise counsel is war waged, and in a multitude of counselors there is safety. 24: 3-6 For a righteous man may fall seven times and rise again, but the wicked shall fall by calamity. V16,17 Prepare your outside work, make it fit for yourself in the field; and afterward build your house. V27

17. It is the glory of God to conceal a matter, but the glory of kings is to search out a matter. 25:2,3 Debate your case with your neighbor, and do not disclose the secret to another; lest he who hears it expose your shame, and your reputation be ruined. V9,10 11 A word fitly spoken is like apples of gold in settings of silver.. V11 By long

forbearance a ruler is persuaded, and a gentle tongue breaks a bone. V15

18. Like a flitting sparrow, like a flying swallow, so a curse without cause shall not alight. 26:2 Do not answer a fool according to his folly, lest you also be like him. Answer a fool as his folly deserves, that he not be wise in his own eyes. V4,5. Where there is no talebearer, strife ceases. V20,21

19. Do not boast about tomorrow, for you do not know what a day may bring forth. 27:1 As iron sharpens iron, so a man sharpens the countenance of his friend. V17 The refining pot is for silver and the furnace for gold, and a man is valued by what others say of him. V21 Be diligent to know the state of your flocks and attend to your herds. V23 The wicked flee when no one pursues, but the righteous are bold as a lion. 28:1 He who trusts in his own heart is a fool, but whoever walks wisely will be delivered. V25,26

20. A fool vents all his feelings, but a wise man holds them back. 29:11 Where there is no revelation, the people cast off restraint; but happy is he who keeps the law. 18 Do you see a man hasty in his words? There is more hope for a fool than for him. 20 A man's pride will bring him low, but the humble in spirit will retain honor. 23 The fear of man brings a snare, but whoever trusts in the LORD shall be safe. 24-26 Who can find an excellent wife? For her worth is far above rubies. The heart of her husband safely trusts her; so he will have no lack of gain. She does him good and not evil all the days of her life. She opens her mouth with wisdom, and on her tongue is the law of kindness. She watches over the ways of her household and does not eat the bread of idleness. Her children rise up and call her blessed; her husband also, and he praises her. 31:26-28

CHAPTER 6

PURPOSE

1. Then God said, 'Let the earth bring forth grass, the herb that yields seed according to its kind, and the fruit tree that yields fruit, whose seed is in itself;' and it was so. And God saw that it was good. Gen 1:11-13 Yet, before any plant of the field was in the earth and any herb of the field had grown, the Lord had not caused it to rain on the earth, and there was no man to till the ground. Gen 2:5 So God said, 'Let Us make man in Our image, and let them have dominion over all the earth.' Gen 1:26 And while the earth remains, seedtime and harvest, cold and heat, winter and summer, day and night shall not cease. Gen 8:22 He has made everything beautiful in its time. He has also put eternity in their hearts, except no one can grasp the work God does from beginning to end. Eccl 3:11 Till the Spirit is poured out from on high, and the desert becomes a fertile field, and the fertile field seems like a forest, justice will dwell in the desert and righteousness live in the fertile field. The fruit of righteousness will be peace; the effect of righteousness will be quietness and confidence forever. Isa 32:15-18

2. Now the Lord said to Abram, "Get out of your country, from your family and from your father's house, to a land that I will show you. I will make you a great nation; I will

bless you and make your name great; and you shall be a blessing. I will bless those who bless you, and I will curse those who curse you; and in you all the families of the earth will be blessed. Gen 12:1-3 So, God helps His servant Israel, in remembrance of His mercy, as He spoke to our fathers, to Abraham and to his seed forever. Luke 1:54-55 Through them came the true Light which gives light to every man coming into the world. John 1:9 So if you are Christ's, then you are Abraham's seed, and heirs according to the promise. Gal 3:29 Therefore bear fruit worthy of repentance and do not say, 'We have Abraham as our father." God is able to raise up children to Abraham from these stones. Even now the axe is laid to the root of the trees. Luke 3:8-9

3. Now, behold the proud. He enlarges his desires as hell. He is like death and cannot be satisfied. Because you have plundered many nations, the remnant of the people shall plunder you! Woe to him who covets evil gain for his house; to set his nest on high; to be delivered from the power of disaster. Giving shameful counsel in his own house; sinning against his own soul. Woe to him who builds with bloodshed and establishes with iniquity. For the earth will be filled with the knowledge of the glory of God!! Hab 2:4-13 Behold, one shall fly like an eagle, and spread his wings over Moab. The strongholds are surprised; mighty men's hearts will be like the heart of a woman in birth pangs. They shall be destroyed as a people, because they exalted themselves against the LORD. Fear and the pit and the snare shall be upon you. He who flees from the fear shall fall into the pit, and he who gets out of the pit shall be caught in the snare. For upon you I will bring punishment. Those who fled stood under the shadow because of exhaustion. But a fire shall come to devour the brow of Moab, the crown of the head of the sons of tumult. Jer 48:40-46

4. Through deceit they refuse to know Me, says the LORD. "Behold, I will refine them and try them; as I deal with the

[slain] of My people. Their tongue is an arrow shot out; it speaks deceit; they speak peaceably to their neighbor with their mouth, but in their heart they lie in wait. Shall I not punish them for these things? Shall I not avenge Myself on such a people as this?" (Jer 9:6-9) They defile their sanctuaries with their many sins and dishonest trade. So the Lord will bring fire from within them, to consume them. He will let it burn them to ashes on the ground in the sight of all watching. All who know them will be appalled at their fate. They have come to a terrible end, and are no more. (Ez 28: 18)

5. This is an evil generation. It seeks a sign, and no sign will be given except the sign of Jonah. For as Jonah became a sign to the Ninevites, so also the Son of Man will be to this generation. The queen of the South will rise up in the judgment with the men of this generation and condemn them, for she came from the ends of the earth to hear the wisdom of Solomon; and indeed a greater than Solomon is here. The men of Nineveh will rise up in the judgment with this generation and condemn it, for they repented at the preaching of Jonah; and indeed a greater than Jonah is here. Luke 11:29-30

6. You do not know what manner of spirit you are of. For the Son of Man did not come to destroy men's lives but to save them. Luke 10:41-42 Every kingdom divided against itself is brought to desolation, and a house divided against a house falls. If Satan also is divided against himself, how will his kingdom stand? You say I cast out demons by Beelzebub. If so, by whom do your sons cast them out? They will be your judges. But if I cast out demons with the finger of God, surely the kingdom of God has come upon you. When a strong man, fully armed, guards his own palace, his goods are in peace. Yet when a stronger than he comes and overcomes him, he takes from him all his armor in which he trusted, and divides his spoils. He who is not with Me is against Me, and he who does not gather with Me scatters. Luke 11:19-23

7. No one puts a piece from a new garment on an old one; otherwise the new makes a tear and the piece that was taken out of the new does not match the old. No one puts new wine into old wineskins; or else the new wine will burst the wineskins and be spilled, and the wineskins will be ruined. New wine must be put into new wineskins, and both are preserved. So no one, having drunk old wine, immediately desires new; for he says, 'The old is better.' Luke 5:36-39 So, when they ran out of wine, the mother of Jesus said to Him, "They have no wine." Jesus said to her, "Woman, what does your concern have to do with Me? My hour has not yet come." His mother said to the servants, "Whatever He says to you, do it." John 2:3-5

8. No prophet is accepted in his own country. Many widows were in Israel in the days of Elijah, when the heaven was shut up and there was a great famine; but to none of them was Elijah sent except to a widow in Zarephath. Many lepers were in Israel in the time of Elisha, and none was cleansed except Naaman the Syrian. Lk 4:24-27 Then He said to Simon, "I entered your house and you gave Me no water for My feet, but this woman has washed My feet with her tears and wiped them with her hair. You gave Me no kiss, but this woman has not ceased to kiss My feet. You did not anoint My head with oil, but this woman has anointed My feet with fragrant oil. Her sins, which are many, are forgiven, for she loved much. But to whom little is forgiven, the same loves little." Luke 7:44-47 This is the condemnation, that the light has come into the world, and men loved darkness rather than light, because their deeds were evil. For everyone practicing evil hates the light and does not come to the light, lest his deeds be exposed. But he who does the truth comes to the light, that his deeds may be clearly seen, that they have been done in God. John 3:19-21

9. He must increase, but I must decrease. He who is of the earth is earthly. He who comes from above is above

all. And what He has seen and heard, He testifies; and no one receives His testimony. He certifies that God is true. For He whom God has sent speaks the words of God, for God does not give the Spirit by measure. The Father loves the Son, and has given all things into His hand. He who believes in the Son has everlasting life; and he who does not believe the Son shall not see life, for the wrath of God abides on him. John 3:30-36 The hour is coming when you will neither on this mountain, nor in Jerusalem worship the Father. You worship what you do not know. We know what we worship, for salvation is of the Jews. But the hour is coming and now is, when true worshipers will worship the Father in spirit and truth. God is Spirit, and those who worship Him must worship in spirit and truth. John 4:21-24 Jesus answered him saying, "Because I said to you, 'I saw you under the fig tree,' do you believe? You will see greater things than these." "Hereafter, you shall see heaven open, and the angels of God ascending and descending upon the Son of Man." John 1:50-51

10. For as the Father raises the dead and gives life to them, even so the Son gives life to whom He will. For the Father judges no one, but has given all judgment to the Son, that all should honor the Son just as they honor the Father. John 5:21-23 No one takes this honor to himself, but he who is called by God, just as Aaron was. Heb 5:4 The hour is coming and now is, when the dead will hear the voice of the Son of God; and those who hear will live. For as the Father has life in Himself, so He has granted the Son to have life in Himself, and has given Him authority to execute judgment also, because He is the Son of Man. Do not marvel at this; for the hour is coming in which all who are in the graves will hear His voice and come forth; those who have done good, to the resurrection of life, and those who have done evil, to the resurrection of condemnation. I can of Myself do nothing. As I hear, I judge; and My judgment is righteous, because

I do not seek My own will but the will of the Father who sent Me. John 5:25-30

11. The works that I do in My Father's name, they bear witness of Me. But you do not believe, because you are not of My sheep. My sheep hear My voice, and I know them, and they follow Me. And I give them eternal life, and they shall never perish; neither shall anyone snatch them out of My hand. My Father, who has given them to Me, is greater than all; and no one is able to snatch them out of My Father's hand. I and My Father are one." John 10:25-30 And I will pray the Father, and He will give you another Helper, that He may abide with you forever, the Spirit of truth, whom the world cannot receive, because it neither sees Him nor knows Him; but you know Him, for He dwells with you and will be in you. John 14:16-18 And when He has come, He will convict the world of sin, and of righteousness, and of judgment: of sin, because they do not believe in Me; of righteousness, because I go to My Father and you see Me no more; of judgment, because the ruler of this world is judged. John 16:8-11

12. So, if you will hear His voice, do not harden your hearts as in the days in the wilderness when your fathers tested Me, and saw My works forty years. I was angry with that generation, and said, 'they always go astray in their heart, not knowing My ways.' So I swore they would not enter My rest. Heb 3:7-11 I traverse the paths of righteousness, in the midst of the paths of justice, that I may cause those who love me to inherit wealth, that I may fill their treasuries. Prov 8: 20-21 He who speaks from himself seeks his own glory; but He who seeks the glory of the One who sent Him is true, and no unrighteousness is in Him. John 7:18-19 So Jesus said to them, Peace to you! As the Father has sent Me, I also send you. Then He breathed on them and said, Receive the Holy Spirit. If you forgive the sins of any, they are forgiven; if you retain the sins of any, they are retained. John 20:21-23

SECTION III

THE STRATEGY

CHAPTER 7

THE MANTLE

1. Lord, what is man, that You take thought of him? Yet You have made him a little lower than God. You crown him with glory and majesty and have made him to rule over the works of Your hands. Ps 8:6 For creation itself longs for the revealing of the sons of God that it might be delivered from the bondage of corruption as it gains entrance into this glorious freedom. For we know that all creation groans and labors with birth pangs together until now. Rom 8:19-22

2. Yet still these people draw near with their mouths and honor Me with their lips, but have removed their hearts far from Me, and their fear toward Me is taught by the precepts of men; therefore, I will again do a marvelous work among this people, a marvelous work and a wonder. For I will destroy the wisdom of the wise and bring to nothing the cleverness of the clever. Woe to those who devise their plans and deny the Lord. Yet in a very little while the barren land shall become a fruitful field, and the fruitful field will be as a forest. In that day the deaf shall hear the truth, and the eyes of the blind shall see. The joy of the humble will increase and the poor shall rejoice in the Holy One of Israel. Isa 29: 14-19

3. You have not yet struggled and resisted to the point of pouring out your own blood. Heb 12:4 For this reason also the wisdom of God said, I will send them prophets and apostles, of whom they will put to death and persecute, that the blood of all the prophets, which was shed from the foundation of the world, may be required of this generation. Luke 11:49, 50 But we have this treasure in earthen vessels, that the excellence of the power may be of God and not of us. We are hard-pressed on every side, yet not crushed; we are perplexed, but not in despair; persecuted, but not forsaken; struck down, but not destroyed—always carrying about in this body the dying of the Lord Jesus, that the life of Jesus also may be manifested in our body. For we who live are always delivered to death for Jesus' sake, that the life of Jesus also may be manifested in our mortal flesh. So then death is working in us, but life in you. 2 Corinthians 4:7-11

4. Why are you so foolish? Having begun by the Spirit, are you now being perfected by the flesh? So then, does He who provides you with the Spirit and works miracles among you, do it by the works of the Law, or by the hearing with faith? Gal 3:3,5. Thus says the LORD: Cursed is the one who trusts in man, who depends on flesh for his strength and whose heart turns aside from the LORD. He will be like a bush in the wastelands; and shall not see when prosperity comes. But blessed is the man who trusts in the LORD, whose confidence is in him. He will be like a tree planted by the waters that sends out its roots by the stream. It does not fear when the heat comes; its leaves stay green. It has no worries in the year of drought and never fails to bear fruit. Jer 17:5-8

5. So if you listen carefully to the voice of the LORD your God and do what is right in his eyes, if you pay attention to his commands and keep all his decrees; I will not bring on you any of the diseases that were brought on the Egyptians, for I am the LORD, who heals you. Ex 15:26. Worship the LORD your God, and I will take away sick-

ness from among you. Ex 23:25 Surely he took up our infirmities and carried our sorrows, yet we considered him stricken by God, smitten by him, and afflicted. But he was pierced for our transgressions, he was crushed for our iniquities; the punishment that brought us peace was upon him, and by his stripes we are healed. Is 53:4,5.

6. The Spirit of the LORD is upon me, because the LORD has anointed me to preach good news to the poor. He has sent me to heal the brokenhearted, to proclaim liberty to the captives and release from darkness for the prisoners, to proclaim the year of the Lord's favor and the day of vengeance of our God, to comfort all who mourn and provide for those who grieve in Zion;. to give them beauty for ashes, the oil of gladness for mourning, and a garment of praise for the spirit of despair. They will be called oaks of righteousness, a planting of the LORD for the display of his splendor. Is 61:1-3

7. He sent forth his word and healed them and delivered them from destruction. Ps 107:20 God is not a man, that he should lie, nor a son of man, that he should change his mind. Does he speak and then not act? Does he promise and not fulfill? Num 23:19. He stood between the living and the dead, and the plague stopped. Num 16:48 When Jesus saw the large crowd, he had compassion on them and healed their sick. Matt 14:14 The demon-possessed were brought to him, and he drove out the spirits with a word and healed all the sick. This was to fulfill what was spoken by the prophet Isaiah: He took up our infirmities and carried our diseases. Matt 8:16, 17. So Jesus went throughout all Galilee, teaching in their synagogues, preaching the good news of the kingdom, and healing every disease and sickness among the people. Matt 4:23

8. It is the Spirit who gives life. God is Spirit and they that know Him must know Him in spirit and in truth. John 6:63, 4:24 So, Jesus said: The Son can do nothing by himself, he can do only what he sees his Father doing because whatever the Father does the Son also does. For the

Father loves the Son and shows him all that he does. To your amazement he will show you greater things than these. John 5:19,20 I am the vine; you are the branches. Whoever abides in me and I in him, he will bear much fruit; apart from me you can do nothing. If you abide in me and my words abide in you, ask whatever you wish, and it will be given you. John 15:5,7 So, whatever you bind on earth will be bound in heaven, and whatever you loose on earth will be loosed in heaven. Mt 18:18 So, behold! I have given you authority to trample upon serpents and scorpions, and over all the power of the enemy and nothing shall by any means harm you. Luke 10:19

9. The centurion answered and said, "Lord, I am not worthy that You should come under my roof. But only speak the word, and my servant will be healed. For I also am a man under authority, having soldiers under me. And I say to this one, 'Go,' and he goes; and to another, 'Come,' and he comes." When Jesus heard it, He marveled, and said to those who followed, "I have not found such great faith, not even in all of Israel! Mat 8:8-10 Anyone who has faith in me will do what I have been doing. He will do even greater things than these, because I am going to the Father. And I will do whatever you ask in my name, so that the Son may bring glory to the Father. John 14:12-14. When Jesus had called the Twelve together, he gave them power and authority to drive out all demons and to heal diseases, and he sent them out to preach the kingdom of God and to heal the sick. Luke 9:1,2

10. God anointed Jesus of Nazareth with the Holy Spirit and power. He went around doing good and healing all who were under power of the devil, because God was with him. Acts 10:38 For this purpose the Son of God was manifested, that He might destroy the works of the devil. 1 John 3:8b Now this is the confidence that we have in Him, that if we ask anything according to His will, He hears us. So if we know that He hears us, whatever we

ask, we know that we have the petitions that we have asked of Him. 5:14, 15

11. Beloved, I pray that you may prosper in all things and be in health, just as your soul prospers. 3 John 1:2 Is anyone among you afflicted or suffering evil? Then he must pray. Is anyone happy? He is to sing praises. Is anyone among you sick? Then he must call for the elders and they are to pray over him, anointing him with oil in the name of the Lord; and the prayer offered in faith will restore the one who is sick, and the Lord will raise him up, and if he has committed sins, they will be forgiven him. Therefore, confess your sins to one another, and pray for one another so that you may be healed. The fervent, effective prayer of a righteous man can accomplish much. Elijah was a man with a nature like ours, and he prayed earnestly that it would not rain, and it did not rain for three years and six months. Then he prayed again, and the sky poured rain and the earth produced its fruit. James 5:13-18

12. Let not let your hearts be troubled. Trust in God; trust also in me. John 14:1 For when two or three come together in my name, there am I in their midst. Matt 18:20 Jesus said, have faith in God. If anyone says to this mountain, 'Go, throw yourself into the sea,' and does not doubt in his heart but believes that what he says will happen, it will be done for him. Whatever you ask for in prayer, believe that you have received, and it will be yours. Mark 11:22-24 The multitudes with one accord heeded the things spoken by Philip, hearing and seeing the miracles which he did. For unclean spirits, crying with a loud voice, came out of many who were possessed; and many who were paralyzed and lame were healed so that there was great joy in that city. Acts 8:6-8 For Jesus Christ is the same yesterday, today and forever. Heb 13:8

13. Ask of me of things to come concerning My sons; and concerning the work of My hands, command you Me. Isa 45:11 Then Jesus said, all authority in heaven and on

earth has been given to me. Go therefore and make disciples of all nations; teaching them to observe all I have commanded you. Matt 28:18 These signs will accompany those who believe: in my name they will drive out demons and speak in new tongues; they will lay hands on the sick and they will recover. So, the disciples went out and preached everywhere and the Lord worked with them confirming his word by the signs that followed. Mark 16:16-20 And the hand of the Lord was with them and great numbers believed and turned to the Lord. Acts 11:21

14. Now an angel of the Lord stood by him, and a light shone in the prison; and his chains fell off his hands. Then the angel said to him, "Follow me." So he followed him, and did not know that what was being done by the angel was real. When they were past the first and the second guard posts, they came to the iron gate that leads to the city, which opened to them of its own accord; and immediately the angel departed from him. Acts 12:7-10 Then Saul, filled with the Holy Spirit, looked intently at the sorcerer and said, "You who are full of all deceit and all fraud, you son of the devil, you enemy of all righteousness, will you not cease perverting the straight ways of the Lord? And now, indeed, the hand of the Lord is upon you, and you shall be blind, not seeing for a time." Acts 13:6

15. To Shebna, I will throw you away violently and there you will die. 'Then it shall be in that day, that I will call My servant Eliakim. I will clothe him with your robe and strengthen him with your belt; I will commit your responsibility into his hand. He shall be a father to the inhabitants of Jerusalem and to the house of Judah. The key of the house of David I will lay on his shoulder; so he shall open, and no one shall shut; and he shall shut, and no one shall open. I will fasten him as a peg in a secure place, and he will become a glorious throne to his father's house. 'They will hang on him all the glory of his father's house.'" Is 22:15-23

16. The wilderness and the wasteland shall be glad and the desert shall rejoice and bloom. They shall see the glory of the Lord, the excellency of our God. So, strengthen the weak hands, and make firm the feeble knees. Say to those who are fearful-hearted, "Be strong, do not fear!" Then the eyes of the blind shall be opened, and the ears of the deaf shall be unstopped. Then the lame shall leap like a deer, and the tongue of the dumb sing. For waters shall burst forth in the wilderness, and streams in the desert. The parched ground shall become a pool and the thirsty land springs of water. A highway shall be there and a road, and it shall be called the Highway of Holiness. The unclean shall not pass over it, for it shall be for the redeemed. Whoever walks this road shall not go astray. Isaiah 35:6-8

CHAPTER 8

DOMINION

1. Come to Me, all you who labor and are heavy laden, and I will give you rest. Take My yoke upon you and learn from Me, for I am gentle and lowly in heart, and you will find rest for your souls. For My yoke is easy and My burden is light. Mt 11:28-30 He who finds his life will lose it, and he who loses his life for My sake will find it. Mt 10: 39 Whoever receives this little child in My name receives Me; and whoever receives Me receives Him who sent Me. For he who is least among you will be greatest. Lk 9:48 Whoever exalts himself will be humbled, and he who humbles himself will be exalted. Mt 23:12 Let no one deceive himself. If anyone among you seems to be wise in this age, let him become a fool that he may become wise. 1 Cor 3:18 So I take pleasure in weaknesses, in needs, in reproaches, in persecutions, in distresses for Christ's sake. For when I am weak, then I am strong. 2 Cor 12:10 I say to you, unless a grain of wheat falls into the ground and dies, it remains alone; but if it dies, it produces much fruit. He who loves his life will lose it, and he who hates his life in this world will keep it for eternal life. John 12:24-25

2. Stepping into one of the boats, Jesus asked Simon its owner, to push out into the water. So he sat in the boat

and taught the people. When they resumed their work, the nets became so full they began to tear. Luke 5:2,3 Jesus said, 'give and it will be given unto you, just as you want people to treat you, treat them in the same way.; Lk 6 Unto him that much is given, much is required; and to whom men have committed much, of him they will ask the more. Lk 5:6,7 Gentile rulers lord over them and their great ones wield their authority. Not so with you. Let him who is the greatest become the least, and the leader as the servant. For I am among you to serve. Lk 22:25-27 Well done, good and faithful servant. You were faithful over a few things, I will make you ruler over many. Mt 25:18

3. She considers a field and buys it, out of her earnings she plants a vineyard. She sets about her work vigorously. She sees that her trading is profitable and her lamp does not go out at night. Prov 31:14-18 Command those who are rich in this present world not to be arrogant or to put their hope in wealth, which is so uncertain; but to put their hope in God, who richly provides us with everything for our enjoyment. Command them to do good, to be rich in good deeds and acts of kindness, and to be generous and willing to share. In this way they will lay up treasure for themselves as a firm foundation for the coming age, so that they may take hold of the life that is truly life. 1 Tim 6:17-19 What does the Lord require of you but to do justly, and to love kindness and mercy, and to humble yourself and walk in humility with your God. Micah 6:8

4. The LORD was with Joseph and showed him mercy, and gave him favor in the sight of the keeper of the prison. Gen 39:21 The Lord will grant this people favor in the sight of the Egyptians; so that when you go, you will not go empty-handed. Exodus 3:21. Moreover Moses was very great in the land of Egypt, in the sight of Pharaoh's servants and in the sight of the people, so that the LORD gave His people favor in the sight of the Egyptians. Ex 11:3 There was not one city that made peace with Israel.

So Israel took them all in battle. For it was of the LORD to harden their hearts that they should come against Israel in battle, that the Lord might utterly destroy them, and that they might receive no mercy, but that the Lord might destroy them, as He had commanded Moses. Josh 11:20 So when Job prayed for his friends, the LORD restored his fortunes and gave him twice as much as before! Job 42:10

5. The land you are entering to take over is not like the land of Egypt from which you have come, where you planted your seed and irrigated it by foot as in a vegetable garden. But the land you are crossing the Jordan to take possession of is a land of mountains and valleys that drinks rain from heaven. It is a land the LORD your God cares for; for the eyes of the LORD your God are continually on it from the beginning of the year to its end. Deut 11:10-12 You have not passed this way before. So, consecrate yourself, for the Lord will do wonders among you. Josh 3:4-5 So Joshua did as Moses told him and fought with Amalek. Moses, Aaron, and Hur were at the top of the hill. When Moses held up his hand, Israel prevailed. But Moses grew weary and Aaron and Hur held up his hands and so Joshua overwhelmed Amalek. Ex 17:10-13 Shout for joy from the mountaintops; give glory to the Lord; for the Lord will go forth like a warrior and arouse His zeal like a man of war and prevail against His enemies. Is 42:11-13

6. Let them not be put to shame, but with all boldness, may Jesus now, as always, be exalted. Adonai, make them one and give them favor in the sight of those who oppose and oppress them. Count them worthy of their calling, and fulfill every desire for goodness and the work of faith with power, so the name of Jesus may be glorified in them, and they in You, according to your grace, O God, and Messiah Jesus. Th 1:11,12 Let your Word, spread rapidly and be glorified. Deliver them from perverse and evil men. Reverse every curse assigned against them.

Expose and remove infiltrators and counterfeits. Direct their hearts into the love of God and steadfastness of Messiah. II Th 3:5 Strengthen them with all power with your glorious might, so they may attain steadfastness and patience joyously. Col 1:11 Open multiple doors for Your Word, so they may speak forth the mystery of Messiah. Col 4:3 Stabilize their times. Knit our hearts in oneness with these our brethren and raise up an army of saints to stand in the gap on their behalf. John 17:23 So dear God of peace, Who brought up from the dead the great Shepherd of the sheep, thru the blood of the eternal covenant, equip them in every good thing to do your will. Heb 13:20 Meet their every need according to Your riches in glory. Phil 4:19 Work in them that which is pleasing in Your sight, through Jesus to Whom be glory forever and ever. Heb 13:21

7. If this plan or this work is of men, it will come to nothing; but if it is of God, it cannot be overthrown; lest those who try be found to fight with God. Acts 5: 38-39 When the Lord restored the captivity of Zion, we were like those who dream. Our mouths were filled with laughter and our tongues with singing. They said among the nations, "The Lord has done great things for them." The Lord HAS done great things for us; and we are glad. Restore us from our captivity, O Lord, as with the streams in the desert. For those who sow in tears shall reap in joy and shall doubt- less come again with rejoicing, bringing in the sheaves with them. Ps 126 Houses and fields and vineyards shall again be bought in this land. So buy for yourself the field, for behold, I am the Lord God of all flesh, is anything too hard for Me? Jer 32:15, 25-27 So He gave them the lands of the Gentiles and they inherited the labor of the nations! Ps 105: 44 For the Lord longs to be gracious to us and indeed rises to show us compassion. Is 30:18

8. Do not charge your brother interest, whether on money or food or anything else. You may charge a foreigner interest, but not a brother, so that the LORD your God

may bless you in everything you put your hand to in the land you are entering to possess. Deut 23:19, 20 Do not take advantage of a hired man who is poor and needy, whether he is a brother or a foreigner living in one of your towns. Pay him his wages on time, because he is poor and counting on it. Otherwise he may cry out to the LORD against you. When you are harvesting your field and overlook a sheaf, do not go back to get it. Leave it for the foreigner, the fatherless and the widow, so that the LORD may bless you in all the work of your hands. When you beat the olives from your trees or harvest the grapes in your vineyards, do not go over the branches a second time. Deut 24: 14-15, 18-21

9. Holy Father, keep us in Your name, the name which You have given to the Lord Jesus, that we may be one, even as You are one. I do not ask that You take us out of the world, but keep us from the evil one. Sanctify us in Your truth. Your Word is truth. Make us one, even as You are one, that the world may know that Jesus the Messiah was indeed sent by You as Savior and Lord. The glory You have given to the Lord Jesus, to Yeshua, we receive, as He gives it to us, for the purpose of being one, just as You are one. We believe that Jesus the Messiah is in us, and You are in Him, and that we will be perfected in unity, so that the world will see that we are objects of Your love, as Jesus the Messiah is the object of Your love. We ask for the Holy Spirit's anointing and infilling in order that we might go into the world into which our Lord has sent us, to minister, to give our lives a ransom for many, to seek and to save that which is lost and to do Your Holy will. John 17: 11,15,16,20-23

10. Lord God, will You not judge them? For we have no power against this force coming against us; nor do we know what to do, but our eyes are upon You. Now all Judah stood before the LORD. And when Jehosaphat had consulted with the people, he appointed those who should sing to the LORD and praise the beauty of holi-

ness. So as they faced their enemy, they repeated: 'Praise the Name of the LORD, for His mercy endures forever.' And as they began to sing and to praise, the LORD set ambushes against their enemies and so they were defeated. 2 Chr 20: 12,13,21,22 The Lord thunders with His majestic voice and does not restrain the lightning when His voice is heard. The Lord thunders wondrously with His voice, doing great things beyond our comprehension. Job 37:4

11. David encouraged and strengthened himself in the Lord his God and inquired of the Lord. The Lord answered David: pursue, for you will surely recover all. So David recovered all; nothing was missing, plus he captured all the enemy's herds. 1 Sam 30: 6,8,18,20 Then Gideon and his men came to the camp in the middle watch and blew the shofars and cried the sword of the Lord and of Gideon. And as they stood their ground, all the Midianites cried out and fled. So Gideon sent messengers throughout all the land, saying, come down against the Midianites and take before them the waters. Judg 7:19-22 Have you entered the treasury of snow or have you seen the storehouse of hail which I have reserved for the time of trouble, for the day of battle and war? Job 38: 22,23 For the LORD has opened His armory, and brought out the weapons of His indignation; for this is the work of the Lord God of hosts. Jer 50:25

12. The poor man's wisdom is despised and his are words not heard. The words of the wise, spoken quietly will be heard rather than the shout of fools. Ec 9:16, 17 The angel said, 'Your prayers have been heard and your alms remembered in the sight of God.' Acts 10:31 For the secret things belong to the LORD, but those that are revealed belong to us and to our children forever. Deut 29:29 Lord, You have given me wisdom and might, and have now made known to me what I asked of You; for there is a God in heaven who reveals secrets and has made known these things. Dan 2:23,28 The people who

walked in darkness have seen a great light; and upon those who have dwelt in the shadow of death, a light has shined. Lord, You have multiplied this nation and increased its joy; so they will rejoice before you according to the joy of the harvest as in the day of Midian. Is 9:2-4 Hear the word of the Lord, for my people Israel. For they will soon come and I will multiply them in the sight of the nations. Ez 36:1-10 I will bring them into the land and cleanse them and give them a new heart and put a new spirit within them. Then the nations around you will know that I am the Lord. I the Lord have spoken it and I will do it. Ez 36:24-27, 36 Forgetting what lies behind and reaching forward to what lies ahead, I press on toward the goal for the prize of the upward call of God in Christ Jesus. Phil 3:13-14 To this end I labor, striving according to His power which works in me mightily. Col 1:29

CHAPTER 9

LIGHT TO THE NATIONS

1. Behold, the days are coming, declares the LORD, when I will make a new covenant with the house of Israel and with the house of Judah, not like the covenant which I made with their fathers in the day I brought them out of the land of Egypt; My covenant which they broke, although I was a husband to them. But this is the covenant which I will make with the house of Israel in these days, I will put My law within them and on their heart I will write it; and I will be their God, and they shall be My people. They will not teach again, each man his neighbor and his brother, saying, 'Know the LORD,' for they will all know Me, from the least of them to the greatest; declares the LORD, for I will forgive their iniquity, and their sin I will remember no more. Jeremiah 31:31-34

2. When they went from one nation to another, from one kingdom to another, He permitted no one to do them wrong. He rebuked kings for their sakes, saying, "Do not touch My anointed ones, and do My prophets no harm." Ps 105:12-15 For they that erred in spirit shall come to understanding, and they that murmured shall learn doctrine. Zech 2: 5 Is 29:24 For I, myself, will be a wall of fire around Jerusalem, says the LORD. And I will be the glory inside the city! On your walls, O Jerusalem, I

have appointed watchmen; all day and all night they will never keep silent. You who remind the Lord, take no rest and give Him no rest until He establishes and makes Jerusalem a praise in the earth. Is 62:6,7

3. Remember, O Lord, the word You commanded Your servant Moses: 'If you are unfaithful, I will scatter you among the nations; but if you return to Me, and keep My commandments and do them, though some of you were cast out to the farthest part of the heavens, yet I will gather you from there, and bring you to the place which I have chosen as a dwelling for My name.' "Now Lord, these are Your servants and Your people, whom You have redeemed by Your great power and strong hand. O Lord, I pray, please let Your ear be attentive to my prayer and to those who desire to fear Your name; and let me prosper this day and grant me mercy in the sight of this man." Neh 1:5-11

4. If you have run with footmen and they have wearied you, then how can you contend with horses? If in the land of peace in which you trusted, they wearied you then how will you do in the floodplain of the Jordan? Jer 12:5 Yet I will lift up My hand to the nations and set up My standard to the peoples; and they will bring your sons in their bosoms, and your daughters will be carried on their shoulders. Kings will be your guardians, and their princesses your nurses and you will know that I am the Lord. Is 49:22 Sing aloud to God our strength, for this is a statute for Israel. This He established in Joseph as a testimony, when he went through the land of Egypt. I called in trouble and You delivered me. You answered me in the secret place of thunder. Psalm 81:1-7

5. They wandered in the wilderness in a desolate way; they found no city to dwell in. Hungry and thirsty, their soul fainted in them. Then they cried to the LORD in their trouble, and He delivered them out of their distresses. He led them forth by the right way, that they might go to a city for a dwelling place. Oh, that men would give thanks

to the LORD for His goodness, and for His wonderful works to the children of men! For He satisfies the longing soul, and fills the hungry soul with goodness. Ps 107: 4-9

6. They sat in darkness and in the shadow of death, bound in affliction and irons; because they rebelled against the words of God, and despised the counsel of the Most High. Therefore He brought down their heart with labor. They fell down, and there was none to help. Then they cried out to the LORD in their trouble, and He saved them out of their distresses. He brought them out of darkness and the shadow of death, and broke their chains in pieces. Oh, that men would give thanks to the LORD for His goodness, and for His wonderful works to the children of men! For He has broken the gates of bronze, and cut the bars of iron in two. Psalm 107:10-19

7. Fools, because of their transgression, and because of their iniquities, were afflicted. Their soul abhorred all manner of food, and they drew near to the gates of death. Then they cried out to the LORD in their trouble, and He saved them out of their distresses. He sent His word and healed them, and delivered them from their destructions. Oh, that men would give thanks to the LORD for His goodness, and for His wonderful works to the children of men! Let them sacrifice the sacrifices of thanksgiving, and declare His works with rejoicing. Psalm 107:17-22

8. Those who go down to the sea in ships, who do business on great waters, they see the works of the LORD, and His wonders in the deep. For He commands and raises the stormy wind, which lifts up the waves of the sea. They mount up to the heavens, they go down again to the depths; their soul melts because of trouble. They reel to and fro and stagger like drunken men, and are at their wits' end. Then they cry out to the LORD in their trouble and He brings them out of their distresses. He calms the storm, so that its waves are still. Then they are glad because they are quiet; so He guides them to their desired haven. Oh, that men would give thanks to the

LORD for His goodness and for His wonderful works to the children of men! Let them exalt Him in the assembly of the people, and praise Him in the company of the elders. Ps 107:23-32

9. He turns rivers into a wilderness and the watersprings into dry ground; a fruitful land into barrenness, for the wickedness of those who dwell in it. He turns a wilderness into pools of water, and dry land into watersprings. There He makes the hungry dwell, that they may establish a city for a dwelling place and sow fields and plant vineyards, that they may yield a fruitful harvest. He also blesses them, and they multiply greatly; and He does not let their cattle decrease. When they are diminished and brought low through oppression, affliction and sorrow, He pours contempt on princes, and causes them to wander in the wilderness where there is no way; Yet He sets the poor on high, far from affliction, and makes their families like a flock. The righteous see it and rejoice and all iniquity stops its mouth. Whoever is wise will observe these things, and they will understand the lovingkindness of the LORD. Psalm 107:33-43

10. Lord, You will not allow my feet to slip. You Who keep Israel neither slumber nor sleep. I know and have heard that You, the everlasting God, the Lord, the Creator of the ends of the earth, do not become weary or tired. Your understanding is inscrutable. You give strength to the weary, and to him who lacks might, You increase power. Ps 121:3, 4 Those who wait on You O Lord, will gain new strength. We will mount up with wings like eagles. We will run and not be weary, we will walk and not faint. Isa 40:24 Your Word that goes forth from your mouth will not return to You empty without accomplishing what You desire and succeeding in the matter for which You sent it. I will go out in joy and be led forth in peace. Isa 55: 8-12

11. The one who sits on the throne as king, must copy these laws for himself in a book. He must always keep this copy of the law with him and read it daily as long as

he lives. That way he will learn to fear the LORD his God by obeying all the words of the law. This regular reading will prevent him from becoming proud and acting as if he is above his people. It will also prevent him from turning away from God's Word in the smallest way. Deut 17:18-20

12. If you follow my ways and obey my requirements, then you will be given authority over my work. I will let you walk in and out of my presence along with these others standing here. You are symbols of the good things to come. Zech 3: 7 So as they were burying a man, they suddenly spied a band of raiders; and they put the man in the tomb of Elisha and when the man was let down and touched the bones of Elisha, he revived and stood on his feet. (2 Kings 13:21) Now God worked unusual miracles by the hands of Paul, Acts 19:11

13. So great fear came upon all the church and upon all who heard these things. And through the hands of the apostles many signs and wonders were done among the people. They were all with one accord in Solomon's Porch and the people esteemed them highly. Believers were increasingly added to the Lord, multitudes of both men and women, so that they brought the sick out into the streets and laid them on beds and couches, that at least the shadow of Peter passing by might fall on some of them. Acts 5:11-15

14. As the Philistines drew near to battle against Israel, the LORD thundered with a loud thunder upon the Philistines and so confused them that they were overcome before Israel. 1 Sam 7: 10 So the LORD spoke to Moses face to face, as a man speaks to his friend. Exodus 33:11 Because you have obeyed my command to persevere, I will protect you from the great time of testing that will come upon the earth to test those who belong to this world. Rev 3:10

15. Lord, You have heard me this day and will preserve me and give me for a covenant to the people. For I will not

go out in haste or by flight, for the Lord will go before me, and the God of Israel will be my rear guard. Is 52:12 My eyes will behold a land of wide distances that stretches afar. I will see no more the fierce and the insolent. But there the Lord will be in majesty and splendor. Is 33: 19-21 So I am steadfast, immovable, always abounding in the work of the Lord, knowing that my labor is not in vain in the Lord. (I Cor 15:58) For God gives wisdom and knowledge and joy to a man who is good in His sight; but to the sinner He gives the work of gathering and collecting, that he may give to him who is good before God. Eccl 2: 26

SECTION IV

THE GOAL

CHAPTER 10

THE REALITIES

1. Let your light so shine before men, that they may see
    your good works and glorify your Father in heaven. Do
    not think I came to destroy the Law or the Prophets, but
    to fulfill. Till heaven and earth pass away not one jot nor
    tittle will pass from the law till all is fulfilled. Whoever
    breaks one of the least of these commandments and
    teaches men so, shall be called least in the kingdom of
    God; but who ever does and teaches them, he shall be
    called great. Unless your righteousness exceeds the
    scribes and Pharisees, you will by no means enter the
    kingdom of God. Matt 5:16-20 Not many should presume
    to be teachers, because we who teach will be judged
    more strictly. Jam 3:1 When the tempter came to Him,
    he said, if You are the Son of God, command that these
    stones become bread. He answered, It is written, 'Man
    shall not live by bread alone, but by every word that pro-
    ceeds from the mouth of God.' Then he took Him up into
    the holy city, set Him on the pinnacle of the temple, and
    said, if You are the Son of God, throw Yourself down. For
    it is written: 'He shall give His angels charge over you,
    and, in their hands they shall bear you up. Jesus said, it
    is written, 'You shall not tempt the LORD your God.' The
    devil took Him up on a high mountain and showed Him

all the kingdoms of the world and their glory. He said to Him, all these things I will give You if You will worship me. Jesus said to him, away with you, Satan! For it is written, You shall worship the LORD your God, and Him only you shall serve. 'So the devil left Him and angels came and ministered to Him. Matt 4:3-11

2. When Jesus heard that John had been put in prison, He departed to Galilee and dwelt in Capernaum, that what Isaiah spoke might be fulfilled: The people who sat in darkness have seen a great light, and for those in the shadow of death, Light has dawned. From that time Jesus began to preach: repent, for the kingdom of heaven is at hand. Matt 4:12-17 Blessed are the poor in spirit, for theirs is the kingdom of heaven. Blessed are those who mourn, for they shall be comforted. Blessed are the meek, for they shall inherit the earth. Blessed are those who hunger and thirst for righteousness, for they shall be filled. Blessed are the merciful, as they shall obtain mercy. Blessed are the pure in heart, for they shall see God. Blessed are the peacemakers, for they shall be called sons of God. Blessed are those who are persecuted for righteousness' sake, for theirs is the kingdom of heaven. Blessed are you when they revile and persecute and say all kinds of evil against you falsely for My sake. Rejoice and be exceedingly glad, for great is your reward in heaven, for so they persecuted the prophets before you. Matt 5:3-12

3. So I say to you, do not worry about your life, what you eat or drink; nor about your body, what you put on. Is not life more than food and the body more than clothing? Look at the birds of the air, for they neither sow nor reap nor gather into barns; yet your heavenly Father feeds them. Are you not of more value than they? Which of you by worrying can add a cubit to his stature? Consider the lilies of the field, how they grow: they neither toil nor spin; and yet I say to you that even Solomon in all his glory was not arrayed like one of these. Now if God so clothes

the grass of the field, which today is, and tomorrow is burned, will He not much more clothe you, O you of little faith? So do not worry, saying, 'What shall we eat?' or 'What shall we drink?' or 'What shall we wear?' For the Gentiles seek after these things. But your heavenly Father knows you need them. So seek first the kingdom of God and His righteousness, and all these things shall be added to you. So do not worry about tomorrow, for tomorrow will worry about its own things. Sufficient for the day is its own trouble. Matt 6:25-34

4. While He spoke these things, a ruler came and worshiped Him, saying, "My daughter has just died, but come and lay Your hand on her and she will live." So Jesus followed him. Suddenly, a woman who had a flow of blood for twelve years touched the hem of His garment. For she said to herself, "If only I may touch His garment, I shall be healed." Jesus turned and said, "Be of good cheer, daughter; your faith has made you whole." She was healed from that hour. When Jesus came into the ruler's house and saw the crowd wailing, He said: Make room, for the girl is not dead, but sleeping. They ridiculed Him, but He went in and took her by the hand, and she arose. Matt 9:18-26

5. Go to the lost sheep of the house of Israel. As you go, preach that the kingdom of heaven is at hand. Heal the sick, cleanse lepers, raise the dead, cast out demons. Freely you have received, freely give. Provide neither gold nor silver, nor bag for your journey; for a worker is worthy of his support. Whatever city or town you enter, inquire who is worthy and stay there till you go. When you go into a household, bless it. If it is worthy, give it your blessing of peace. If it is not, let your blessing return to you. Whoever will not receive you nor hear your words, when you depart from that house or city, shake the dust off your feet. It will be more tolerable for Sodom and Gomorrah in the day of judgment than for that city! Matt 10:6-15 You are the salt of the earth; but if the salt

loses its flavor, how shall it season? It is then good for nothing but to be thrown out and trampled underfoot. You are the light of the world. A city set on a hill cannot be hidden. A lamp is not lit and put under a basket, but on a lampstand to give light to all who are in the house. Matt 5:13-15

6. Now brother will deliver up brother to death, and a father his child; and children will rise against parents and cause them to be put to death. You will be hated by all for My name's sake. But he who endures to the end will be saved. When they persecute you in one city, flee to another. A disciple is not above his teacher, nor a servant above his master. If they have called the master of the house Beelzebub, how much more will they call his household! But do not fear them. For there is nothing covered that will not be revealed, and hidden that will not be known. Matt 10:21-26 Whatever I tell you in the dark, speak in the light; and what you hear whispered, shout it from the housetops. Do not fear those who kill the body but cannot kill the soul. Are not two sparrows sold for a penny? Not one of them falls to the ground apart from your Father knowing. The very hairs of your head are numbered. So do not fear; you are of more value than many sparrows. I did not come to bring peace but a sword. For I have come to set a man against his father, a daughter against her mother and a man's enemies will be those of his own household. He who loves father or mother more than Me is not worthy of Me. He who loves son or daughter more than Me is not worthy of Me. He who does not take up his cross and follow after Me is not worthy of Me. He who finds his life will lose it and he who loses his life for My sake will find it. Matt 10: 27-31, 34-39

7. Then He began to rebuke the cities in which most of His miracles had been done, because they did not repent: "Woe to you, Chorazin! Woe to you, Bethsaida! For if the miracles which were done in you had been done in Tyre and Sidon, they would have repented. Capernaum,

who has been exalted to heaven will be brought down to Hades. At that time Jesus prayed, I thank You, Father, Lord of heaven and earth, that You have hidden these things from the wise and prudent and have revealed them to babes. All things have been delivered to Me by My Father, and no one knows the Son except by the Father, nor does anyone know the Father except by the Son. Matt 11:20-27

8. Then the Pharisees said, Your disciples are doing what is not lawful on the Sabbath! But He said, have you not read what David did when he was hungry: how he entered the house of God and with his men ate the show-bread? Or have you not read on the Sabbath the priests in the temple profane the Sabbath and are blameless? If you had known what this means, 'I desire mercy and not sacrifice,' you would not have condemned the guilt-less. For the Son of Man is Lord even of the Sabbath." Matt 12:2-8 Brood of vipers! How can you, being evil, speak good things? For out of the abundance of the heart the mouth speaks. A good man out of the treasure of his heart brings forth good things, and an evil man evil things. So for every idle word men may speak, they will give account in the day of judgment. For by your words you will be justified, and by your words you will be con-demned. Matt 12:34-37

9. When an unclean spirit goes out of a man, he goes through dry places seeking rest and finds none. Then he says, I will return to my house and find it put in order. So he takes with him seven other spirits more wicked to enter to dwell there; and the last state of that man is worse than the first. So shall it also be with this wicked generation. Matt 12:43-45 Woe to the world because of offenses! For offenses must come, but woe to those by whom they come! Take heed that you do not despise one of these little ones, for in heaven their angels always see the face of My Father. For the Son of Man has come to retrieve that which was lost. If a man has a hundred

sheep and one goes astray, does he not leave the ninety-nine to seek the one straying? If he should find it, he rejoices more over that one than the ninety-nine that did not stray. It is not the will of your Father that one of these little ones perish. Matt 18:7-14

10. If your brother sins against you, go alone and tell him his fault. If he hears you, you have gained your brother. But if he will not hear, take one or two more, that 'by the mouth of two or three witnesses every word be established.' If he refuses to hear, tell it to the church. If he still refuses even to hear, let him be to you like a heathen and a tax collector. So whatever you bind on earth will be bound in heaven, and whatever you loose on earth will be loosed in heaven. If two of you agree on earth concerning anything that they ask, it will be done for them by My Father in heaven. For where two or three are gathered in My name, I am there in the midst of them. Matt 18:15-20

11. Jesus went into the temple and drove out those who bought and sold and overturned the tables of money changers. He said, it is written, My house shall be called a house of prayer, but you have made it a den of thieves. Matt 21:12-13 The kingdom of heaven is like a certain king who arranged a wedding for his son. But those invited made light of it and went one to his farm; another to his business. The rest seized his servants and killed them. When the king heard, he was furious. He sent out his armies to destroy the murderers. Then he said to his servants, those invited were not worthy; go into the thoroughfares of the city and as many as you find, invite to the wedding. They gathered all they found, both bad and good. So, the wedding hall was filled. When the king came in, he saw one without a wedding garment and said, 'friend, how did you come without a wedding garment?' He was speechless. Then the king commanded, 'bind him and cast him into outer darkness; there will be weeping and gnashing of teeth.' "For many are called, but few are chosen." Matt 22:2-14

12. Take heed no one deceives you. For many will come in My name, saying, 'I am the Messiah,' and will deceive many. You will hear of wars and rumors of wars. See that you are not troubled; for these things must come to pass, but the end is not yet. For nation will rise against nation, and kingdom against kingdom. There will be famines, pestilences, and earthquakes in various places. These are the beginning of sorrows. They will deliver you up to tribulation and you will be hated by all nations for My name's sake. Many will be offended, betray one another, and hate one another. False prophets will rise up and deceive many. Because lawlessness will abound, the love of many will grow cold. But he who endures to the end shall be saved as this gospel of the kingdom is preached in all the world as a witness to all the nations, and then the end will come. When you see the 'abomination of desolation,' spoken of by Daniel the prophet, standing in the holy place, let those in Judea flee to the mountains. There will be great tribulation, such as has not been since the beginning of the world, no, nor ever shall be. For the elect's sake these days will be shortened. If anyone says, 'Look, here is the Christ!' do not believe it. For false messiahs and false prophets will rise with great signs and wonders to deceive if possible, even the elect. Know, I have told you. Matt 24:4-25

CHAPTER 11

THE STANDARD

1. The LORD said to Moses, "When you go back to Egypt, see that you do all those wonders before Pharaoh which I have put in your hand. Ex 4:21 Enter by the narrow gate; for wide is the gate and broad is the way that leads to destruction and many are those who go in by it. But narrow is the gate and difficult is the way which leads to life, and there are few who find it. Beware of false prophets, who come to you in sheep's clothing, but inwardly are ravenous wolves. You will know them by their fruits. Do men gather grapes from thornbushes or figs from thistles? Even so, every good tree bears good fruit, but a bad tree bears bad fruit. Every tree that does not bear good fruit is cut down and thrown into the fire. Not everyone who says to Me, 'Lord, Lord,' shall enter the kingdom of heaven, but he who does the will of My Father. Many will say to Me, 'Lord, have we not prophesied in Your name, cast out demons and done many wonders in Your name?' I will declare to them, 'I never knew you; depart from Me, you who practice lawlessness! Matt 7:21

2. The wind goes toward the south and turns around to the north; it whirls about continually and comes again on its circuit. Eccl 1:6 Look, I'm sending you out as sheep

among wolves; so be wary and wise as serpents, but as innocent as doves, harmless and without pretense. Be wary of men who will betray you; but know, this will yield opportunity, so do not be anxious, for what you say will be given to you by the Holy Spirit. Matt 10:16-20 So, I say to you, love your enemies, bless those who curse you, do good to those who hate you, and pray for those who spitefully use and persecute you, that you may be sons of your Father in heaven; for He makes the sun rise on the evil and on the good, and sends rain on the just and the unjust. Matt 5:44, 45

3. Teach them the statutes and principles and show them the way in which they must walk and the work they must do. Then select from all the people able men, such as fear God, men of truth, hating covetousness; and place them as rulers of thousands, of hundreds and fifties, and of tens. Ex 18:20, 21 The Lord will bless you and increase your numbers. He will bless the fruit of your womb, the crops of your land—the calves of your herds in the land that he swore to your forefathers to give you. You will be blessed more than any other people. Deut 7:13, 14 There should be no poor among you, for in the land the LORD your God is giving you to possess, he will richly bless you. For the LORD your God will bless you as he has promised, and you will lend to many nations but will borrow from none. You will rule over many nations but none will rule over you. Deut 15:4, 6

4. If there is a poor man among your brothers, do not be hard-hearted or tight-fisted towards your poor brother. Rather be open-handed and freely lend him whatever he needs. Give generously without a grudging heart; so the LORD will bless you in all the work of your hands. There will always be poor people in the land. So, I command you to be open-handed towards your brothers and towards the poor and needy in your land. Deut 15: 7-11 13 For this is the will of God, that by doing good you may put to silence the ignorance of foolish men. 1 Peter 2:15

So then, while we have opportunity, let us do good to all people, but especially to those who are of the household of the faith. Gal 6:10 Silver and gold have I none, but such as I have, I give to you; in the Name of Jesus, get up and walk! Acts 3:6 Out of the most severe trial their overflowing joy and extreme poverty welled up in rich generosity so that they gave beyond their ability. 2 Cor 8:2,3

5. Ask, and it will be given to you; seek, and you will find; knock, and it will be opened to you. For everyone who asks receives, and he who seeks finds, and to him who knocks it will be opened. What man among you if his son asks for bread, will give him a stone? Or if he asks for a fish, will give him a serpent? If you then, being evil, know how to give good gifts to your children, how much more will your Father in heaven give good things to those who ask Him! Behold, a sower went out to sow. So, as he sowed, some seed fell by the wayside and the birds came and devoured it. Some fell on stony ground, where it did not have much earth; and immediately it sprang up and was scorched by the sun and withered away because it had no root. Some seed fell among thorns; and the thorns grew up and choked it, and it yielded no crop. But then there was seed that fell on good ground and yielded a crop that increased and produced: some thirtyfold, some sixty, and some a hundred. Mark 4: 3-8

6. Take heed what you hear. With the same measure you use, it will be measured to you; and to you who hear, more will be given. For whoever has, to him more will be given; but whoever does not have, even what he has will be taken away. Mark 4: 24-25 In whatever place you enter to stay, stay till you depart from that place. And whoever will not receive you nor hear you, when you depart, shake off the dust from under your feet as a testimony against them. Mark 6:10, 11 Do not give what is holy to the dogs; nor cast your pearls before swine, lest they trample them and turn and tear you to pieces.

So they will set out to discourage and make you afraid to go on building. Yet, they will have no part with you in building this work. You alone will build it as has been commanded. Ezra 4:3-4

7. Yet, he who is not against us is on our side. For whoever gives you a cup of water in My name, will by no means lose his reward. So, learn to recognize those who labor among you. 1 Thes 5:12 But whoever causes one of these little ones who believe in Me to stumble, it would be better if a millstone were hung around his neck and he were thrown into the sea. For everyone will be seasoned with fire, and every sacrifice will be seasoned with salt. Salt is good, but if the salt loses its flavor, how will you season it? Have salt in yourselves and peace with one another." Mark 9: 40-42, 49-50 There is no one who has left house or brothers or sisters or father or mother or wife or children or lands for My sake and the gospel's who shall not receive a hundredfold now in this age, with persecutions—and in the age to come, eternal life. But many who are first will be last and the last first. Mark 10: 29-31 So, judge not, that you be not judged. For with what judgment you judge, you will be judged; and with the measure you use, it will be measured back to you. And why do you look at the speck in your brother's eye, but do not consider the plank in your own? First remove the plank from your own eye, and then you will see clearly to remove the speck from your brother's. Matt 7:1-3

8. So, when you pray, don't be like the hypocrites. They love to pray standing in the synagogues and on the corners of the streets, that they may be seen by men. They have their reward. But when you pray, go into your room, and when you have shut your door, pray to your Father who is in the secret place; and your Father who sees in secret will reward you openly. Matt 6:5, 6 Beware of those who love greetings in the marketplaces, the best seats in the synagogues, and the best places at feasts, who devour widows' houses, and for a pretense make long prayers.

Mk 12: 38-40 When the first came, they supposed that they would receive more. When they had received the same, they complained saying, 'These last men have worked only one hour, and we have borne the burden and the heat of the day.' But he answered, 'Friend, did you not agree on this amount? Take what is yours and go your way. I wish to give this last man the same as you. Is it not lawful for me to do what I wish with what I own? Or is your eye evil because I am good?' So the last will be first, and the first last. For many are called, but few chosen. Matt 20: 10-16

9. A fire shall come to devour the sons of tumult. Fear and the pit and the snare shall be upon you, says the Lord. He who flees from the fear shall fall into the pit, and he who gets out of the pit shall be caught in the snare. Jer 48:40-42 When King Jeroboam heard the man of God, he stretched out his hand, saying, "Seize him!" Then his hand withered and the altar was split apart. Then the king cried, "Please entreat the Lord's favor and pray for me, that my hand may be restored." So his hand was restored. Then the king said, "Come home with me and I will give you a reward." But the man of God said to the king, the Lord commanded me not eat bread, nor drink water, nor return by the same way. So he left by another route from the way he came to Bethel. On the way, an old prophet came to him and said, "Come home with me and eat bread, for I too am a prophet and an angel spoke to me to bring you back to my house. So, as they sat at the table, the word of the LORD came to the old prophet and he cried out, saying, "Thus says the LORD: 'Because you have disobeyed the word of the LORD, ate bread, and drank water, your corpse shall not come to the tomb of your fathers.'" 1 Kings 13:4-22

10. When I turned to see who was speaking to me, I saw seven gold lampstands and in their midst was the Son of Man. He was wearing a long robe with a gold sash. His head and hair were white as snow. His eyes were bright

like flames of fire. His feet were as refined bronze, and his voice thundered like mighty ocean waves. He held seven stars in his right hand, and a sharp two-edged sword in his mouth. His face was as bright as the sun. When I saw him, I fell at His feet. He laid His right hand on me and said, "Fear not! I am the First and the Last, the living one who died. Now, I am alive forevermore! I hold the keys of death and the grave. The seven stars are the angels of the seven churches, and the lampstands are the churches. Rev 1:12-20

11. To the church in Thyatira. I know all the things you do—your love, your faith, your service, and your endurance. I see your constant improvement. But I have this against you. You are permitting that Jezebel who calls herself a prophet—to lead my servants astray. She is encouraging spiritual seduction and idolatry. I gave her time to repent, but she would not turn away from her immorality. So, she will suffer greatly with all those seduced by her, unless they turn away from their evil deeds. I will strike her children dead. All the churches will know that I am the one who searches the thoughts and intents of the heart. Each will be given whatever they deserve. I also have a message for the rest of you who have not followed this doctrine. Hold tightly to what you have until I come. To all who are victorious, who obey me to the end, I will give authority over the nations. You will rule the nations with an iron rod and have the same authority I received from my Father, and I will also give you the morning star! Rev 2:18-29

12. To the church in Philadelphia from the one who is holy and true, who has the key of David. He opens doors that no one can shut; he shuts doors that no one can open. I know all the things you do, and I have opened a door for you that no one can shut. You have little strength, yet have obeyed my word and did not deny me. So, I will force those who belong to Satan—those liars who say they are Jews but are not—to come and bow down at

your feet. They will acknowledge that you are the ones I love. Because you have obeyed my command to persevere, I will protect you from the great time of testing that will come upon all the earth. I am coming quickly. So, hold fast to what you have, so that no one takes away your crown. All who are victorious will become pillars in God's Temple and will never have to leave it. I will write God's name on them and they will be citizens in God's city—the new Jerusalem that comes down from heaven. They will have my new name inscribed upon them. Rev 3:7-13

CHAPTER 12

THE KINGDOM

1. When you see a cloud rising in the west, you say, 'A shower is coming'; and so it is. When you see the south wind blow, you say, 'There will be hot weather'; and there is. So, why do you discern the face of the sky and the earth, but not the times? Lk 12 These things I have spoken to you, that My joy may be in you, and your joy may be made full. Jn 15:11 Until now you have asked for nothing in My name; ask, and you will receive, that your joy may be made full. Jn 16:24 Well done, good and faithful servant; you were faithful over a few things, I will make you ruler over many. Enter into the joy of your lord. Matt 25:21-22 This hope is an anchor of the soul, both sure and steadfast which enters within the veil, where Jesus has entered as a forerunner for us, having become a high priest forever according to the order of Melchizedek. Heb 6:19-29 My servant Caleb, because he has a different spirit and has followed Me fully, I will bring into the land and his descendants shall possess it. Num 14:24

2. Repent, for the Kingdom of Heaven is at hand. Matt 5:3 Blessed are those who are persecuted for righteousness sake, for theirs is the Kingdom of Heaven. Matt 5:10 Your Kingdom come, Your will be done on earth as it is in

heaven. Matt 6:10 Yours is the Kingdom and the power and glory forever. Matt 6:13 Seek first the Kingdom of God and His righteousness and all these other things will be added to you. Matt 6:33 Jesus went about all the cities and villages, teaching in their synagogues, preaching the gospel of the kingdom, and healing every sickness and disease among the people. Matt 9:35 From the days of John the Baptist until now the kingdom of heaven suffers violence, and the violent take it by force. Matt 11:12 It has been given to you to know the mysteries of the kingdom of heaven, but to them it has not been given. For whoever has, to him more will be given, and he will have abundance; but whoever does not have, even what he has will be taken away from him. Matt 13:11-12

3. When anyone hears the word of the kingdom, and does not understand it, then the wicked one comes and snatches away what was sown in his heart. Matt 13:19 The kingdom of heaven is like a man who sowed good seed in his field; but while his men slept, his enemy came and sowed tares among the wheat and went his way. Matt 13:24-26 The kingdom of heaven is like a mustard seed, which a man sowed in his field, which indeed is the least of all the seeds; but when it is grown it is greater than the herbs and becomes a tree, so that the birds of the air come and nest in its branches. Matt 13:31-32 The kingdom of heaven is like leaven, which a woman took and hid in a large amount of flour until it permeated into dough. Matt 13:33 The Son of Man will send out His angels, and they will gather out of His kingdom all things that offend, and those who practice lawlessness, and will cast them into the furnace of fire. Then the righteous will shine forth as the sun in the kingdom of their Father. Matt 13: 41-43

4. The kingdom of heaven is like treasure hidden in a field, which a man found and hid. For joy over it he goes and sells all that he has and buys that field. Matt 13:44 The kingdom of heaven is like a merchant seeking beautiful

pearls, who when he had found a pearl of great value, went and sold all that he had and bought it. Matt 13:45-46 The kingdom of heaven is like a net cast into the sea that gathered some of every kind. When it was full, they sat down and gathered together the good, but threw the bad away. Matt 13:47-49 I will give you the keys of the kingdom of heaven, and whatever you bind on earth will be bound in heaven, and whatever you loose on earth will be loosed in heaven. Matt 16:19 There are some standing here who shall not taste death till they see the Son of Man coming in His kingdom. Matt 16:28

5. Unless you are converted and become as little children, you will by no means enter the kingdom of heaven. Therefore whoever humbles himself as this little child is the greatest in the kingdom of heaven. Matt 18:3-5 The kingdom of heaven is like a certain king who wanted to settle accounts with his servants. One was brought to him who owed him ten thousand talents. He was not able to pay, so his master commanded that he be sold, with his family and all that he had that the payment be made. The servant fell down, saying, 'Master, have patience with me, and I will pay you all.' Then the king was moved with compassion, released him, and forgave him the debt. But the servant refused to forgive his fellow servants their debts, so the king was angry and delivered him to the prison until he paid all. Matt 18:23-27

6. A man had two sons, and he came to the first and said, 'Son, go, work today in my vineyard.' He answered and said, 'I will not,' but afterward he regretted it and went. Then he came to the second son and said likewise. He answered him, 'I go, sir,' but he did not go. Which of the two did the will of his father? They said to Him, 'The first.' So Jesus said to them, surely, tax collectors and harlots will enter the kingdom of God before you. Matt 21: 28-31 Therefore, the kingdom of God will be taken from you and given to a people bearing the fruits of it. Matt 21:43-44 But woe to you, scribes and Pharisees, hypocrites! For

you shut up the kingdom of heaven against men; for you neither go in yourselves, nor do you allow those who are entering to go in. Matt 23:13-14 This gospel of the kingdom will be preached in all the world as a witness to all the nations and then the end will come. Matt 24:14

7.   The kingdom of heaven shall be likened to ten virgins who took their lamps and went out to meet the bridegroom. Five of them were wise and five were foolish. Matt 25:1-3 The kingdom of heaven is like a man traveling to a far country, who called his servants together and delivered his goods to them. To one he gave five talents, to another two, and to another one, to each according to his own ability; and then he went on his journey. Matt 25:14-16 Then the King will say to those on His right hand, 'Come, you blessed of My Father, inherit the kingdom prepared for you from the foundation of the world: for I was hungry and you gave Me food; I was thirsty and you gave Me drink; I was a stranger and you took Me in; I was naked and you clothed Me; I was sick and you visited Me; I was in prison and you came to Me.' Then the righteous will answer Him, saying, 'Lord, when did we feed You, take You in, or clothe You? He will answer them, 'In as much as you did it to one of the least of these My brethren, you did it to Me.' Matt 25:37-46

8.   Do you not know that to whom you present yourselves as slaves to obey, you are that one's slaves? God be thanked that though you were slaves of sin, yet you wholeheart- edly obeyed the teaching in which you were entrusted. Having then been set free from sin, you became slaves of righteousness. Rom 6:16-18 Do not destroy with your food him for whom Christ died nor let what is for you a good thing be spoken of as evil; for the kingdom of God is not eating and drinking, but righteousness and peace and joy in the Holy Spirit. Rom 14:15-18 Therefore I take pleasure in weaknesses, in reproaches, in difficulties, in persecutions, in distresses, for Christ's sake. For when I am weak, then I am strong. 2 Cor 12:10 So lest I should

be exalted above measure by the abundance of the revelations, a thorn in the flesh was given to me, a messenger of Satan to buffet me. I pleaded with the Lord three times that it might depart from me. And He said to me, "My grace is sufficient for you, for My strength is made perfect in weakness." Therefore most gladly I will rather boast in my weaknesses, that the power of Christ may rest upon me. 2 Cor 12:7-9

9. For the Lord GOD will help me; therefore I will not be disgraced; therefore I have set My face like a flint, and I know I will not be ashamed. He is near who justifies me; so who will contend with me? Let us stand together. Who is my accuser? Let him come near me. For the Lord GOD will help me; so that those who condemn me will be like an old garment; that the moth has eaten away. Is 50:7-9 Who have you reproached, against whom have you raised your voice and lifted up your eyes on high? Against the Holy One of Israel. I know your dwelling place: your going out and your coming in, and your rage against Me. Because your rage against Me and your tumult have come up to My ears, so I will put My hook in your nose and My bridle in your lips, and I will turn you back by the way which you came. Isaiah 37: 28,29

10. God's household, having been built upon the foundation of the apostles and prophets, Jesus Himself being the corner stone, is growing into a holy temple in the Lord; in whom you also are being fitted together into a dwelling of God in the Spirit. Eph 2:19-22 The mystery of Christ, of the Gentiles being joint heirs of the promises of the gospel, has now been revealed by the Spirit to God's holy apostles and prophets. Eph 3:4-5 Unto you that fear His Name shall the Sun of Righteousness arise with healing in His wings, and you shall go forth and grow up as calves of the stall. Mal 4:2 Through the tender mercies of our God; whereby the Dayspring from on high has visited us; to give light to those who sit in darkness and

the shadow of death, to guide our feet into the way of peace. Lk 1:79

11. Unto us a Son is given; and the government will be upon His shoulder. His name will be called Wonderful, Counselor, Mighty God, Everlasting Father, Prince of Peace. Of the increase of His government and peace there will be no end. He will reign on the throne of David and over His kingdom to order it and establish it with judgment and justice from that time forward, even forever. The zeal of the Lord of hosts will perform this. Is 9:6-7 He shall not judge by the sight of His eyes, nor decide by the hearing of His ears; but with righteousness He shall judge the poor, and decide with equity for the meek of the earth; He shall strike the earth with the rod of His mouth, and with the breath of His lips He shall slay the wicked. Righteousness shall be the girdle of His loins, and faithfulness the belt of His waist. Is 11:3-4 Then the kingdoms of this world will become the kingdoms of our Lord and he shall reign for ever. Rev.21: 10

12. Then righteousness will dwell in the desert and the desert will become a fertile field and the fertile field seems like a forest. The fruit of righteousness will be peace, and the effect of righteousness, quietness and confidence forever. How blessed you will be sowing your seed beside every stream; letting your herds range free. Isa 32: 15, 20 The sinners in Zion will be terrified; trembling will grip the godless. For who can dwell with the consuming fire? It is he who walks righteously and speaks uprightly, who rejects gain from extortion and keeps his hand from accepting bribes, who shuts his eyes to considering evil — this is the man who will dwell on the heights, whose refuge will be the mountain fortress. His bread will be supplied and water will not fail him. Isaiah 33: 14-16 I am the LORD your God, Who teaches you to profit, Who leads you by the way you should go. Isaiah 48:17 So, I will contend with those who contend with you, and I will save your children. I will feed those who oppress you

with their own flesh, and they shall be drunk with their own blood. Then all will know that I, the LORD, am your Savior, and your Redeemer, the Mighty One of Jacob. Isaiah 49:25-26

CONCLUSION

SPIRITUAL TRACTION

"You enlarged my path under me; so my feet did not slip." 2 Sam 22:37

With these times has come a manifestation of seducing, lying religious spirits. The distractions, confusion and uncertainty they generate are masking realities on which major Kingdom decisions are being made. As many modern-day Josephs and Daniels are at the point of releasing strategic agendas, the result is "choking up," "stalling out" and creating slippage of these efforts.

Restoring the momentum will require the release of "something more," a dimension extending beyond natural abilities and human effort.

Long before becoming king, against all odds, David challenged and defeated the giant Goliath. In so doing, David stepped into a realm beyond his natural abilities. With his life and the future of Israel on the line, David entered an arena of oneness with the Lord that pierced the spiritual veil. He turned what seemed a hopeless situation into a gateway of opportunity for all of Israel, as well as himself.

Years later, after many feats in battle as king, in 2 Samuel 21:15 David and his men were again fighting giants among the Philistines. During one particular clash, the scripture tells us that David grew faint with one of the sons of the giants moving in to kill him. At that critical point, Abishai came to David's aid, killing the Philistine giant. Then David's men admonished him, saying, *"You shall go out no more with us to battle, lest you quench the lamp of Israel."*

In this encounter, David was enticed into presuming on the success he had previously wielded against the Philistines. He overlooked getting his direction and strategy afresh from the Lord. The result was that he was overwhelmed and apart from the valiant intervention of Abishai, his future as king, along with Israel's destiny would have been short-circuited.

The Seduction

Religious spirits specialize in infiltrating the ranks of the successful among God's people to undermine and derail. Their modus operandi carries a potent seductiveness. They impersonate and mimic the Spirit's intentions, but like David's near fatal skirmish with the giants, they provoke myopic exertions that divert, counterfeit and fall short of the Spirit's big-picture intentions.

The current plague of distracting religious spirits appeals to a "purist" expectation of perfection, when reality calls for simplicity and movement, which will bring forth the alignment required for the impending birthing.

Sophisticated Snares

The schemes that entrap, trip up and create slippage to those stewarding strategic agendas are subtle. They mask an almost indiscernible fine line between soul and Spirit. The seduction of the soul in these instances goes beyond basic issues of righteousness, targeting the wisdom needed to clearly discern the Spirit's guidance.

At the forefront of these schemes are obsessive principles, positional pride, fear of humiliation and illusions of reality. In short, religious spirits bring distortion and perversion into what should otherwise be strengths within a mature believer.

One of my primary mentors used to say that if the devil can't entice you to become lukewarm; he'll get you so red-hot that you're no earthly good. Either way, you've slipped off the narrow path. The quest we each spend a lifetime developing, of doing the right thing right, can become an obsession that distorts ones balance and perceptions in a way that results in *"ever learning and never coming to the knowledge of truth."*

A man I worked with some years ago embraced some of the highest principles I have ever seen. Together with his sense of excellence, he demonstrated, through his ministry, a dimension of biblical operations few have ever broached. Yet, the extreme nature of his principles was accompanied by an equal level of blind spots that eventually began undermining the core and essence of the significant impact he had developed. The scheme is one of being entrapped in a delusion of self-righteousness, as was evidenced by the oppressive mandates of the Pharisees in Jesus' day.

"Hypocrites, for you shut up the kingdom of heaven against men; for you neither go in yourselves, nor do you allow those who are entering to go in." Matt 23:14

Overlapping this stratagem is one reflected by a ministry associate I heard described as belonging to a "tribe of peacocks." The description of this "tribe" of leaders reflected ones "who have been groomed to be peacocks; and when they come out 'among us,' they preen themselves to display their peacock splendor; and in so doing let you know that they deserve to be peacocks." This ministry associate is incredibly accomplished in the work of his calling. However this perversion of positional pride represents a serious weakness in the infrastructure of his accomplishments. The seduction is in *"thinking more highly of ourselves than we ought."* *"Then I will take away those who rejoice in pride and I will leave in your midst a meek and humble people, and they shall trust in the name of the LORD."* Zeph 3:11-12

Strongly related to these snares is the fear of humiliation. This devious fear creates behavior that distorts and destabilizes the foundations of what might otherwise become a great work for the Lord. At its center is the concern with the approval of men rather than giving prime focus to God's approval. True humility is based on one flowing within a foundation of it *"no longer being us, but Christ who lives within us."* Avoiding this subtle scheme represents a deep and abiding trust in the Lord. *"He who speaks from himself seeks his own glory; but He who seeks the glory of the One who sent Him is true, and no unrighteousness is in Him."* John 7:18-19

Deceiving the Elect

Obsessive principles, positional pride and fear of humiliation are each examples of diabolical traps used to seduce the soul of the mature. Jesus warned that in the last days, the enemy's schemes would be designed to deceive even the very elect. They entail pushing what is good to extremes and making it perverse. Applied against ones wielding the mantles birthing strategic agendas, they involve riding the wave of past successes; creating increasingly greater pressures against the soul, until the mind and emotions are overwhelmed.

These and other such schemes lead into distortions of reality that gradually diminish the operation of the Spirit because of being overwhelmed. The result is in crossing a fine line into being dominated by the subtle entrapments of the soul.

Just as maturity is progressive, so stewarding the mantle of one's calling evolves with the bar becoming increasingly higher. The narrow path of the Kingdom takes its practitioners into new levels, as the Spirit leads from faith to faith. It is at these transitions that the impossible become possible. However, these transitions will not succeed through increasing the complexities of human effort or the repetition of past achievements, but by the simplicity defined by the order demonstrated by the Spirit.

Approaching the Gateway

The approach to these new levels will contain a unique "key" or strategy from the Lord; designed not only to open the gateway, but meant to sustain the next level of the pathway. Obtaining this key will require the fine-line discerning and avoidance of the enticements, along with clarity in ascertaining the Lord's strategy.

Not unlike the exhaustion and sense of being overwhelmed that hit David at a critical point in his effort against the son of the Philistine giant, so today many of the ones entrusted with vital initiatives are facing weariness in their well-doing. Preventing the sense of being overwhelmed calls for a special wisdom the Lord spoke to me many years ago: *"Whatever sphere you begin walking into; immediately begin looking beyond it, lest it overwhelm you."*

New arenas demand something fresh and something more, to not only navigate the transition, but to eventually sustain "the new thing." The crucible for release will entail *an approach that has already begun reaching beyond the challenges at hand.*

In the passageway from faith to faith, just repeating what worked in the past may prove to be a snare. In Jesus' earthly ministry, there was a progressive nature to the miracles He performed in raising the dead. From the daughter of the ruler who had just died, to Lazarus who had been buried four days, to His own resurrection, each reflected a unique response along with an increase of its link to the Spirit's power.

Careful discerning of spiritual cycles provides wisdom for avoiding these traps. As there are cycles in the times and seasons, so there are cycles in the realm of the spirit. Defining the boundaries of one's calling within the parameters of the spiritual cycle will release an authority that moves mountains.

The reality is that those with the callings of modern-day Josephs and Daniels need to be operating beyond themselves. Yet too often the inclination, like David's near-fatal encounter with the son of the giant, is to be snagged on the wrong side of the *"dividing asunder between soul and spirit."* That's not to suggest a backslidden state, but rather an increasingly higher standard, along with the need for realistic priorities and balance to release God's intervention. It calls for spiritual traction that conforms with the progressive nature of our callings from faith to faith.

Penetrating the Threshold

The sophistication of the devil's schemes against the mature will be outclassed by God's supernatural strategies. However, that supernatural dimension will only manifest by what was begun in the spirit seeing its conclusion being brought about by the Spirit, rather than by human effort. This means reestablishing the spiritual traction needed to pierce the veil in the realm of the spirit.

Deuteronomy 17: 18-20 bears repeating. As apt guidance needed for leaders and those entrusted with high-level agendas, it admonishes that the one who sits on the throne, the one wielding God's authority, must copy and immerse himself in the Scriptures. He must refresh himself daily in God's Word, as long as he lives.

Memorizing and rehearsing key segments of God's Word represents the catalyst that will bridge the gap of the well-intentioned operation of the soul to release the fire of the supernatural power of the Spirit.

It's not a head-thing. It's a practice that brings the soul into subjection to the spirit. It accompanies the mantle of those anointed, called and entrusted with Joseph-Daniel agendas. It's the something more that releases the authority needed when nothing less than God's intervention will suffice.

It is the brand mark of those anointed to be priestly-kings. Its practice differentiated those kings who would be remembered for good in the generations to come from those who fell short. It is the foundation to the subtle distinction between what we try to do for God and what He allows us to do through Him. It reflects a constant inquiring of the Lord, along with the practice of consecration and a willingness to wait upon the Lord before traction is gained into the new levels of the pathway.

"You've not passed this way before, so consecrate yourselves, for the Lord is about to do wonders among you." Joshua 3:5

This pathway takes a special measure of anointed, Word-washed self control combined with obedient faith to bypass the sophisticated schemes and distance its practitioners from the illusions of reality planted by the enemy of our souls.

"Do not be conformed to the patterns of this world, but be transformed by the renewing of your mind, that you may prove what is that good and acceptable and perfect will of God." Rom 12:2

Word-washed self control maintains the fine-line pathway between soul and spirit which displays the reality of God operating in our midst that the world longs to see. It is the radar in the spiritual guidance system designed to alert and evade the seductive entrapments of the soul bearing on past victories; impulses that play into the devil's array of sophisticated schemes; preliminary impressions of the heart that haven't been sufficiently prayed through; or simply giving heed to perceptions that play into soul-level feelings and ego.

David's encounter with the son of the giant followed all the confusion and disorder of Absalom's unsuccessful overthrow of his throne. David was still overwhelmed and falling short of the mantle of his calling. This near-death skirmish bordered so closely on losing it all for all Israel that punctuated by his men's counsel, it brought David face to face with the spiritual reality needed for entrance into the Spirit's pathway for his kingship.

The result was the "something more" that pierced the spiritual veil to gain what lay ahead. From David's response of a listening and humble heart, came repentance and the spiritual traction that released him into the final steps whereby the throne of David was to become a light to the nations and the one on which the Messiah will reign over His Kingdom.

"You are my lamp, O LORD. The LORD will enlighten my darkness. For by You I can run against a troop; by my God I can leap over a wall. As for God, His way is perfect; the word of the LORD is proven. He is a shield to all who trust in him."
2 Sam 22:29-31

EPILOGUE

BEYOND OURSELVES

"The Spirit of the LORD is upon me, because the LORD has anointed me to preach good news to the poor. He has sent me to heal the brokenhearted, to proclaim freedom for the captives and release from darkness for the prisoners, to proclaim the year of the Lord's favor and the day of vengeance of our God." Isaiah 61: 1-2

This Messianic passage, encompassing a focus uniquely capturing God's heart, reflects key components that pierce the darkness with His Light. They combine to actuate the "something more," the catalyst, that ignites the power needed for societal change. Driven by the Spirit and operating within the spiritual veil beyond ourselves; this dynamic employs the authority and anointing of dominion to bring restoration and transformation.

The Body has been through an intense preparation for what is now on the horizon. In the last generation, the Church that began with a largely disjointed, localized, in-bred, myopic influence is emerging far more mature, connected and mobilized. It is now closing the gap to making a transforming impact on society, reflected by the elements of this prophecy in Isaiah.

The context is a world whereby the perception is considered the reality. It has almost become a tenet of faith that marketing rules the world. Success has become measured by the glitter of the press release, the achievement expectation and the names being dropped.

Yet, from the Torah to the teachings of Jesus is the plumb line for reality. The fullness in this Isaiah 61 passage points to a gate that is narrow, a pathway that is difficult and is focused on the type of service that brings change that carries a cost. It is the "something more" needed in hopelessly dark situations. It is the path that triggers the power to transform when confronting unmasked darkness and embedded evil. It is the pathway of the committed and mature.

True reality will be defined by those Kingdom paradoxes that challenge the wide gate with its self-promotional and manipulative mantras adopted by this age's superstars. Jesus admonished us to get beyond ourselves with the words: *"He who loves his life will lose it."* He went on to call for humility and service as the true indicators of leadership: *"Let he who is greatest among you become the least and the leader as a servant."* Paul likewise addressed the need to overcome the short-sided worldview through which we process reality: *"Whoever thinks he is wise in this age, let him become a fool that he may become wise."*

Expounding on the Torah, Jesus reconnected people to God and mapped out the path that drew a most unlikely band of followers. Under the mantle of the Isaiah 61 prophecy, He established the foundations of reclaiming dominion to bring the change for establishing God's Kingdom.

Collateral Fruit

The dynamic of bearing fruit, of living a life with purpose that makes a difference has long been a mark of the Jewish community. As the forerunner to Jesus' earthly ministry, John the Baptist exhorted his listeners to *"bear fruit worthy of repentance.'* Jesus imparted to his followers the Kingdom dynamic that *"unless a grain of wheat fall into the ground and dies, it remains alone; but if it dies, it bears much fruit."* (John 12:24) In that same vein, Jesus noted that He is the vine and we are the branches. The one who abides in Him will bear much fruit. (John 15:5)

When I set my heart to align with His, there came a simplicity tied to what began unfolding in late 1995 at the onset of my Internet ministry of prayer and writing (SIGN). Already embracing maturity and leadership, this heart-priority led to a process that has taken me beyond myself. What has resulted since that time has been "something more," far exceeding my expectations. It can only be described as collateral fruit birthed from the priority of the alignment with His heart.

This devotional, for example, is part of this collateral fruit. It is the fourth in a series of books that address the leadership dynamic of the Joseph-Daniel calling of those called to change nations. The God's Economy entrepreneurial program is also very much collateral fruit from this focus given to time in His presence, of seeking the priorities of His heart.

With an impact spanning five continents, these joint efforts have mobilized the hopeless with purpose. We equip and establish leaders in their own nations to become catalysts of influence to their communities. The combined thrust between this bottom-up entrepreneurial program and the top-down influence of those being mobilized as modern-day Josephs and Daniels is opening gateways and bringing change to nations.

Specific agendas have varied, but have included entrepreneurial startup programs, mentoring and spiritual business leadership training, along with community building strategies for lands of persecution and oppression. These initiatives are based on the "something more" that is activated through God, despite what appears as hopeless. Within Israel, there has been the opportunity to help organize and launch, and serve as a board member for the Joseph Project, an Israeli-based international consortium of organizations that assists Israeli immigrants and citizens with humanitarian aid.

The Path Bearing Fruit

The people of the world are looking for something more. In the West, there is an emptiness and discontent brought by the seducing illusions of reality and empty trappings of success. There is a nagging awareness of there being a "something more" to it all. In the non-Western world that "something more" too often involves the necessities of life. In both instances people are looking for the reality of God operating in their midst. The narrow path that bears fruit that remains addresses our response to reality, the need for new mind-sets, awareness of the cost of power and the priority of stewardship that bears enduring fruit.

Wisdom provides a beyond-the-superficial response to reality. It reflects a long-term perspective that transcends the blindness of the self-orientation and its consequent dependence on a worldly view of things. It recognizes that the standard to make a difference comes only from a dynamic, prophetic wisdom from on high. The sons of Issachar understood the times and knew what to do. "Knowing what to do," is not based on conforming to the standards of the age, but rather on hearing God and leveraging realistic steps toward the restoration yearned for in the heart of God.

"Whoever thinks he is wise in the age, let him become a fool that he may become wise." 1 Cor 3:18

Jesus' earthly ministry challenged the mind-sets of His followers to respond to the world with the heart of a king. God intended his people to be the head and not the tail. We were never meant to be like everyone else. The Kingdom-minded response is a paradox to the natural way of thinking. The departure of the Kingdom response to persecution, oppression and adversity is captured with the following words:

"Love your enemies, bless those who curse you, do good to those who hate you, and pray for those who spitefully use and persecute you, that you may be sons of your Father in heaven; for He makes the sun rise on the evil and the good and sends rain on the just and the unjust." Matt 5:44, 45

In his second letter to the Corinthians, the Apostle Paul wrote about the exchange required to release the power of God. He spoke of the treasure of our faith and the conflicts that would result from the confrontations of Light and darkness. He simultaneously noted that the cost and impact of imparting Life by the power of the Spirit would result in walking a narrow pathway that would constantly be skirting death.

"We have this treasure in earthen vessels, so that the surpassing greatness of the power will be of God and not from ourselves. We are hard-pressed on every side, yet not crushed; perplexed, but not in despair; persecuted, but not forsaken; struck down, but not destroyed, always carrying about the dying of the Lord Jesus, that the life of Jesus might be manifested." 2 Cor 4:7-10

Since reaching for that "something more," based on the priorities of God's heart, my priorities have changed. The cost has reshaped my pathway. The wonderful opportunities we've embraced across the world are simply the fruit of this path. The path for me has become a lifestyle of arising in the middle of the night to pray and write. It incorporates an annual time alone with the Lord to re-consecrate, to memorize and rehearse scripture and lay the foundation spiritually in prayer for "next steps."

True leadership serves. True service is the stewardship of our gifts, each according to his own ability, to the benefit of the community, based on the priorities of God's heart. Tz'dakah, charitable-righteousness, is the foundation. True service blesses the community. *"Well done, good and faithful servant; you were faithful over a few things, I will make you ruler over many. Enter into the joy of your lord."* Matt 25:21-22

True service bears its own collateral fruit and a type of increase activated only by God. This increase is best described by the word exponential. "Exponential" is an increase of not just adding to something, but doubling, quadrupling or raising a quantity to a multiple of what it was originally. Investing the "combined deposit" of spiritual capital of our individual calling, anointing and gifts properly aligned with His heart, brings results bearing an exponential increase. It is evidence of the process of becoming one with Him. It is the fruit of the obedience to persevere described in Revelation 3:10.

The Lord has called us as agents of change in a time of change. As ambassadors of change, Jesus indicated we would be as sheep among wolves. Within this pressure cooker environment, amid adversity and backlash, is a catalyst to the change. It is the catalyst for the "something more" that only God could bring. Noted by the Isaiah 61 passage, it is the authority for favor.

The Path to Something More

Favor operates at different levels, ranging from the individual to the community, but then at a level that is beyond any human effort.

At the individual level, gateways actuating favor frequently become stepping stones to a higher or a more strategic positioning of those called to bring change. Yet, the more vital function of these gateways of imparting God's blessing, service, and anointed leadership is marked by the first levels of change that in turn lead to the next levels of favor.

At every stage in Joseph's tenure in Egypt, he walked in a favor that defied the odds. As a slave in Potiphar's house, those around him recognized the hand of God in all Joseph did.

"The Lord was with Joseph and he was a successful man and everyone saw that the Lord was with Joseph and made all that he did to prosper." Genesis 39: 2,4

Jesus spoke of going the extra mile. People who are not seen as being out for themselves begin to be trusted. That trust becomes the spiritual capital for favor. When Joseph was in prison, he served. He mastered his own spirit and aligned it with God. He just didn't sit in his cell and sulk. When there was a need, he did what he knew to do and he served. That service brought favor and promotion. Like in Potiphar's house, the jailer promoted Joseph to be his overseer.

"The Lord was with Joseph and showed him mercy and gave him favor in the sight of the keeper of the prison." Genesis 39: 21

The dynamic of community favor was demonstrated by Moses. When oppression reigns, it is apparent to all. So when Moses returned to Egypt as deliverer, the Egyptians, even those in direct service to Pharaoh, took heart in Moses' bold steps. The result was that the Israelites began enjoying favor from the Egyptians around them because of Moses.

"Moreover Moses was very great in the land of Egypt, in the sight of Pharaoh's servants and of the people, so that the Lord gave His people favor in the sight of the Egyptians." Ex 11:3

Likewise, the prayer of Jabez contains the elements needed to confront and dispel darkness at the community level: honor, blessing, enlargement and the authority of the hand of the Lord. The scripture says that Jabez was more honorable than his brothers. Honor is the recognition by the people around you to how you rightly respond to the reality around you. Joseph operated as an honorable man with God always being seen at the forefront in all that he did. Moses, Joseph and Jabez each extended more than just the blessing of God; but the hand of God, which carried the authority to proclaim and bestow those blessings. The result was and will be the driving out of strongholds, accompanied by enlargement.

Establishing Dominion

God created man to rule over the work of His hands. When that endowment of power takes place in cooperation with Him, it releases the blessings of God. Within the "narrow gate," the cycle is nurtured as the blessings of God are freely given. The blessings of God in turn activate a response of favor to the things of God and people of God. That in turn triggers the power for change.

When those in authority over Joseph recognized God's authority operating through him, they entrusted him with their authority. It happened with Potiphar. It continued with the jailer and was the means by which Joseph was promoted to sit along side of Pharaoh. Joseph's promotion then provided the extended influence and authority to bring blessing, not only within Pharaoh's boundaries, but into God's purposes for His chosen for all eternity.

The momentum of favor within the narrow gate will build until it produces an overflow of His presence and power. This overflow will be an unstoppable, consuming fire, that cycles from and then back into sparking the elements of the anointing for dominion and the authority for favor.

This level of favor and divine intervention is infused into impossible and hopelessly dark situations to release results that defy the odds. It is a favor with the authority to proclaim God's dominion in hostile, oppressive environments. It is pivotal to the process of transformation.

This authority will have its foundation in trust and be accompanied with the byproducts of favor: promotion, provision, enlargement, influence and protection. It will be the bread of those paying the cost of embracing His heart. The authority to reverse the stronghold of darkness will see its full release when the people of the world, within the context of their communities, economies and nations, witness the operation of the reality of God; and respond with a favor that unlocks and clears the way. So it will be from the momentum of the bottom-up Isaiah 61 impartations of transformation that the top-down manifestations will ignite.

The Lord's Favor and Set-Times

Historically, previous times of the Lord's favor have been seasons that have brought great change without going completely over the top. This is the first generation approaching both a connected, mobilized, mature Body and a reach that is global in its potential.

The time of the Lord's favor borders on set times; times established by the Father alone (Matt 24:36). As the struggle between the forces of good and evil builds to a climax, the Spirit will release the authority of favor to those traversing the narrow path. It will draw the response of the world, from the least to the great, toward those not just talking the talk, but demonstrating the power of the Lord where darkness has prevailed. With that response will be a release of the "something more," the fire of God that devours corruption, oppression and evil; and brings forth the change that restores His Kingdom.

"Now Lord, these are Your servants and Your people, whom You have redeemed by Your great power and strong hand. O Lord, I pray, please let Your ear be attentive to my prayer and to those who desire to fear Your name; and let us prosper this day and grant us favor..." Nehemiah 1:10-11

APPENDIX

BIBLE READING CHART

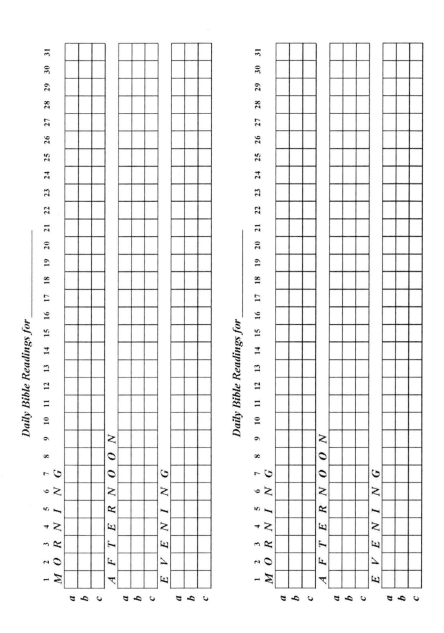

BIBLE READING PLAN

MORNING

SECTION A
	No. of Chapters
Proverbs	31

SECTION B
	No. of Chapters
I Corinthians	16
II Corinthians	13
Galatians	6
Ephesians	6

SECTION C
	No. of Chapters
Genesis	50
Exodus	40
Deuteronomy	34
Joshua	24

AFTERNOON

SECTION A
	No. of Chapters
Psalms	150

SECTION B
	No. of Chapters
Philippians	4
Colossians	4
I Thessalonians	5
II Thessalonians	3
I Timothy	6
II Timothy	4
Titus	3
Philemon	1
Hebrews	13

SECTION C
	No. of Chapters
Judges	21
Ruth	4
I Samuel	31
II Samuel	24
I Kings	22
II Kings	25
I Chronicles	29
II Chronicles	36
Ezra	10
Nehemiah	13
Esther	10
Job	42
Ecclesiastes	12
Song of Solomon	8
Leviticus	27
Numbers	36

EVENING

SECTION A
	No. of Chapters
Matthew	28
Luke	24
Acts	28
Mark	16
John	21

SECTION B
	No of Chapters
Romans	16
James	5
I Peter	5
I John	3
II John	1
III John	1
Jude	1

SECTION C
	No. of Chapters
Isaiah	66
Jeremiah	52
Lamentations	5
Ezekiel	48
Daniel	12
Hosea	14
Joel	3
Amos	9
Obadiah	1
Jonah	4
Micah	7
Nahum	3
Habakkuk	3
Zephaniah	3
Haggai	2
Zechariah	14
Malachi	4

This plan divides the Bible into 9 sections: 5 Old Testament   4 New Testament.

The 9 sections rotate within themselves and you read 1 chapter from each section every day. In the morning you will read a chapter from 2 Old Testament sections and 1 New Testament section (as shown in the A, B and C sections of the morning category. You will do the same for your afternoon. The evening reading will have 2 New Testament and 1 Old Testament chapters in the reading. In other words, you read three chapters three times a day totaling 9 chapters.

This plan will take you through the Old Testament almost twice a year and the New Testament over 5 times a year, along with being in Psalms and Proverbs daily, and the Epistles three times a day. You will be touching upon 9 points of the Bible every day. Every born-again believer must be spiritually fed and this plan gives you a breakfast, lunch and dinner for your spirit every day.

Let Your Soul Delight Itself in Fatness (Isaiah 55:26)

EXAMPLE

	1	2	3	4
MORNING				
Prov				
I Cor	1	2	3	4
Gen	1	2	3	4

PRAYER FOR THE PERSECUTED CHURCH AND THE BELIEVERS IN ISRAEL

I pray that they will not be put to shame in anything, but that with all boldness, Jesus the Messiah shall even now, as always, be exalted. Adonai, make them one and give them favor in the sight of those who oppose and oppress them. May they be counted worthy of their calling, and fulfill every desire for goodness and the work of faith with power, in order that the name of Jesus, of Yeshua may be glorified in them, and, they in You, according to your grace, O God, and Messiah Jesus. (Thes 1:11,12) Let your Word, Lord, spread rapidly and be glorified. May they be delivered from perverse and evil men; and O Lord, reverse every curse assigned against them. Expose and remove infiltrators and counterfeits. Direct their hearts O Lord, into the love of God and steadfastness of Messiah. (II Thes 3:5) Strengthen them, Adonai, with all power according to your glorious might, so they may attain steadfastness and patience joyously. (Col 1:11) Open multiple doors for Your Word, so that they may speak forth the mystery of Messiah. (Col 4:3) Stabilize their times. Knit our hearts in oneness with these our brethren and raise up an army of saints to stand in the gap on their behalf. And dear God of peace, Who brought up from the dead the great Shepherd of the sheep, through the blood of the eternal covenant, even Jesus, Yeshua our Lord; equip them in every good thing to do your will. Meet their every need according to Your riches in glory. Work in them that which is pleasing in Your sight, through Jesus the Messiah, to Whom be the glory forever and ever. Amen!

CLEANSING PRAYER FOR
CLARITY OF HEARING

Lord God, in the Name of Jesus, I come boldly in humility before your throne. Cleanse my heart O God. Thank You that I am cleansed by the blood of Jesus and that the Holy Spirit lives within me. And now, I bring every thought and attitude of my mind along with every impression in my heart into captivity to the obedience of Jesus. Lord, I want to hear what You have to say. I trust You to communicate to me. And in the Name of Jesus, I take authority over every soulish stronghold along with every demonic and interfering spirit. I forbid any enemy activity to operate in my mind or soul. I open my heart to the Holy Spirit — to inspire, to guide, to illuminate and reveal to me truth, insights and perspectives that will anoint my efforts in [this endeavor]. I take authority over fear, anxiety, deception, confusion, doubt and unbelief in the name of Jesus. I bind any negative, deceiving, confusing, critical or condemning spirits in the Name of Jesus and forbid you to interfere with or in any way to imitate God's voice to me. Lord, I thank you for being in charge of every aspect of my being and for all that will unfold in this process. I look forward to what will result from walking in this new dimension with you and for what You have planned for me through it. In the Name of Jesus. Amen

AUTHOR
Morris E. Ruddick

Entrepreneur, consultant, minister and business owner, Morris Ruddick has led development of entrepreneurial activities in critical needy areas and brought together combined business-ministry initiatives in several nations, with a focus on assisting believers in lands of persecution and distress. Mr. Ruddick's Kingdom agendas reflect a unique merging of the secular and the spiritual with initiatives based on biblical principles of business. Since 1995, he has been at the forefront of encouraging and mobilizing spiritually-minded business leaders to step out in faith by combining their entrepreneurial and spiritual gifts to build communities and impact their nations.

In the last few years Mr. Ruddick's Kingdom agendas have spanned five continents with hands-on activities in Russia, Belarus, Nigeria, Ethiopia, Botswana, Afghanistan, China, Vietnam and Israel. His Kingdom business initiatives have included entrepreneurial startup programs, training for spiritual business leaders and community building strategies for lands of persecution and oppression. His programs are based on the biblical model of sowing and reaping in famine. He helped organize and launch, and continues serving as board member for the Joseph Project, an Israeli-based international consortium of humanitarian aid that assists Israeli immigrants and citizens.

Israel's Technology Incubator Program is listed among the clients he has served. He is a former board member of the Nehemiah Fund, an Israeli non-profit (amuta) that has provided grants to members of Israel's believing community facing economic distress.

Mr. Ruddick served 19 years on the board of Marilyn Hickey Ministries and Orchard Road Christian Center where he was Chairman of both the Compensation and Audit Committees. He is a member of the Messianic Jewish Alliance. He served as Corporate Secretary of the International Christian Chamber of Commerce-USA and is a board member of Love Botswana Outreach. He has been a national speaker and workshop leader for the National Religious Broadcasters, Mike and Cindy Jacob's Out of the Box Marketplace Conferences, the GCOWE Missions Conference, Os Hillman's Marketplace Ministry Leader's Summit, Peter Wagner's Roundtable on Kingdom Wealth, the Kingdom Economic Yearly Summit (KEYS); and as a part of the editorial advisory board of the *Journal of Ministry Marketing and Management.*

Over the years, he has served executive suite management with his planning and strategy development talents in a diversity of progressive mid-sized operations, ministry groups, and Fortune 500 companies. He has been at the helm of designing and implementing two successful corporate turn-arounds, one being for a $1.4 billion firm. He holds ordination papers from the United Christian Ministerial Association, a BS from Northwestern University; and an MS in communications and doctoral work in statistics; as well as a year of biblical studies at Oral Roberts University.

CONTACT INFORMATION

To contact the author
to speak at your conference or gathering of
marketplace leaders,
please write

Morris Ruddick
Global Initiatives Foundation
P.O. Box 370291
Denver, CO 80237 USA

or email:

info@strategic-initiatives.org

or call 303.741-9000 and leave a message

You may wish to visit the Global Initiatives Foundation website. It contains additional articles and information.
The website address is:

http://www.strategic-initiatives.org

The Strategic Intercession Global Network (SIGN) and the blogsite for the Strategic Issues Global Network may be found respectively at:
www.strategicintercession.org
http://strategicissuesnetwork.blogspot.com